TEAM BUILDING

TEAM BUILDING

A Sourcebook of Activities for Trainers

GLEN M PARKER & RICHARD P KROPP JR

KOGAN
PAGE

This book is dedicated to our wives, Judy Parker and Barbara Davies, in thanks for their continued support and love.

First published in the United States of America in 1992
© by HTD Press, Amherst, Massachusetts

This UK edition first published in 1992 by Kogan Page

Kogan Page Limited
120 Pentonville Road
London N1 9JN

British Library Cataloguing in Publication Data
A CIP record for this book is available from the British Library.

ISBN 0 7494 0763 8

Printed and bound in Great Britain by
Biddles Ltd, Guildford and King's Lynn

Table of Contents

Introduction 7
A Team Building Process...9
Team Building Intervention Models 10
Index to Activities 11
Activities
  1   Tricky Tales: A Cross-Team Team Building Approach 17
  2   Yea Team!...27
  3   Getting to Know the Boss 31
  4   Robin Hood—An Empowerment Activity............................33
  5   The Ball Game 35
  6   Really . . . But I Thought! 37
  7   Dealing with Problem People on Teams 39
  8   Resolving Intergroup Conflict..43
  9   A Breath of Fresh Air..45
 10   Self Renewal: An Activity for a Mature Team 47
 11   The Car Case 49
 12   Why Are We Here? 53
 13   Skills for Sale 55
 14   TMS—A Process for Role Clarification 57
 15   Characteristics of an Effective Work Team:
       An Assessment Activity 61
 16   Drawings 65
 17   Communicating About Conflict 67
 18   Freeze Frame: Dealing with Problem Behaviours in Teams...............71
 19   My Team and Me 73
 20   Mapping Team Success...77
 21   Darts: A Get Acquainted Activity......................................81
 22   Project "OP"...85
 23   The Victory Tour 89
 24   Creating a Team Mission...95
 25   The Product Development Team...99
 26   Transition Team Building...105
 27   Forming New Teams 107
 28   Linking Team Problem Solving with Corporate Strategy 115

29 Team Building Interview Guide 119
30 Visioning a Vision 123
31 A "Prescription" for Team Effectiveness 125
32 The Team of Your Life 127
33 I Think I Make a Contribution 129
34 Team on Team 133
35 Team Development: A Grid Perspective 137
36 Selecting a Problem Solution 141
37 Selecting a Team Problem 145
38 Project Rescue 149
39 Roadblocks: A Constraint Activity 153
40 The Quality Case: An Ethical Dilemma...................................159
41 Tough Jobs..163
42 Questions We Ask Ourselves 169
43 Team Conflict Mode..173
44 That's Me: A Get Acquainted Activity 177
45 The Effective Team Member: A Consensus Activity 181
46 Creating a Team Logo 187
47 I'm Gonna Sit Right Down and Write Myself a Letter 189
48 Interdependent Images 191
49 SOS: An OD Intervention 193
50 Improving Team Meetings 197

Introduction

What is a Team?

A group of people do not make a team. A team is a group of people with a high degree of interdependence focused on the achievement of some goal or task. The group agrees on the goal and the process for achievement.

The purpose of this collection of activities is to help the team leaders, team building specialists, classroom trainers, and anyone interested in creating collaborative work teams to bring a group of people into harmony and effectiveness.

There are many skills required to be truly effective as a team leader and team developer. This manual provides a collection of activities that can be used with intact work teams or with training groups who will go back to their work environment and build effective teams.

The philosophy that underlies all of the activities in this manual revolves around three key ideas. They are:

1. Each team has a common purpose, mission, or goal.
2. The members are interdependent (they need each other to achieve their purpose).
3. They agree they must work together effectively to reach their goal.

Types of Teams

Many teams meet this definition. The basic work team is a manager and his or her direct reports. Teams can also be ad hoc groups such as task forces or committees which come together for a specific purpose and a limited time. A recent phenomenon is the cross-functional team which brings together experts from a variety of disciplines and departments to develop new products, systems, or other results.

We may distinguish teams by three dimensions:

1. Purpose—product development, quality, marketing, systems, etc.
2. Duration—permanent or ad hoc.
3. Membership—functional or cross-functional.

The most challenging teams are the cross-functional, ad hoc teams. The challenge increases when the purpose is unclear. Although the payoff is potentially great, the difficulty of forging an effective team is complicated by the different styles that the people from the various disciplines bring to the table. And the temporary nature of the relationship often decreases the motivation to work hard on building an effective team.

Team Building and Team Training

Team building is data-based intervention, which assesses the strengths and improvement opportunities of a work team and then prepares and implements plans to increase the effectiveness of the team. Team building also increases the ability of the team to diagnose and solve its own problems.

Team building is often used to describe what we would call training in team effectiveness. Training focuses on increasing the effectiveness of individuals by providing them with skills and knowledge to improve their job performance. Team effectiveness training is, therefore, a programme that increases the ability of people to function as a member or leader of a team.

Participants in a workshop on teamwork may come from a variety of teams. In some instances entire teams may come to a workshop and can benefit from learning together. In these cases, training may approximate team building if the team assesses its effectiveness and uses the learning from the workshop to improve its performance.

Team effectiveness training provides participants with skills and knowledge to increase their personal effectiveness and ultimately the effectiveness of their teams. The training will include topics such as problem-solving, decision-making, communications, goal-setting, meetings management, conflict resolution, research tools, presentation skills, and team success factors.

In this manual we have included activities that can be used in both team building and team training. As appropriate, we distinguish between those activities that are better used in training and those that are more effective in team building.

A TEAM BUILDING PROCESS

STEP 1   The request for a team building process

STEP 2   Develop a contract with the client

STEP 3:   Conduct data gathering relevant to the client's situation using
- interviewing
- questionnaires
- focus groups

STEP 4:   Process and analyse data received and formulate recommendations

STEP 5:   Provide feedback to the client and determine how/if a team building intervention model should be engaged in

STEP 6:   Intervention design and implementation

STEP 7:   Evaluation and follow up

TEAM BUILDING INTERVENTION MODELS

The design of a team building intervention model is dependent upon the organizational context and the purpose of the work teams. Several options are available. We have included two samples for your consideration.

MODEL 1: **Half Day Data Sharing Session**
Intervention Design

STEP 1   Conduct one-to-one interviews with the client and team members.

STEP 2   Hold a team meeting to provide feedback of the one-to-one interviews.

STEP 3   Develop action plans designed to deal with the issues raised, themes presented and problems identified by setting dates and time for follow-up meeting, and assigning action items.

Various exercises in this manual can be used to support this model. For example, Activity 29, Team Building Interview Guide, would be useful in Step 1.

MODEL 2: **Full Day Session on Mission, Purpose and Vision**
Intervention Design

STEP 1   This model is used to help clarify mission, purpose or create a new vision for teams. Again, Step 1 is a data gathering phase intended to uncover the mission, purpose and/or clarify the vision of the team.

STEP 2   Using one of the activities in this manual, write a mission or purpose statement or conduct a visioning exercise. See for example, Activity 24, Creating a Team Mission and Activity 30, Visioning a Vision.

STEP 3   Conduct a focus group regarding the product of Step 2 for feedback.

STEP 4   Build an action plan to implement the product of Step 3.

STEP 5   Establish follow-up plans, dates and times.

The model presented in Model 2 can be modified for such topics as role clarification, team development, problem solving or conflict resolution. The key to successfully using these activities is understanding that they are vehicles for improving performance and increasing the ability of the teams to be self-directed and self-renewing.

INDEX TO ACTIVITIES

No.	TITLE	Page	Ice Breakers	Evaluations	Diagnosis	Team Effectiveness	Skills Building	Conflict Role	Problem Solving	Decision Making	Group Skills	Team Communication	Team Leadership
1	Tricky Tales: A Cross-Team Building Approach	17	•										
2	Yea Team!	27	•										
3	Getting to Know the Boss	31			•								•
4	Robin Hood—An Empowerment Activity	33		•	•	•							
5	The Ball Game	35										•	
6	Really . . . But I Thought!	37			•			•					
7	Dealing with Problem People on Teams	39				•		•	•	•	•		
8	Resolving Intergroup Conflict	43										•	
9	A Breath of Fresh Air	45			•							•	
10	Self Renewal: An Activity for a Mature Team	47		•				•					
11	The Car Case	49								•	•		•
12	Why Are We Here?	53			•				•				
13	Skills for Sale	55					•						
14	TMS—A Process for Role Clarification	57			•			•				•	
15	Characteristics of an Effective Work Team: An Assessment Activity	61		•									•
16	Drawings	65		•				•	•				

11

INDEX TO ACTIVITIES (Continued)

No.	TITLE	Page	Ice Breakers	Evaluations	Diagnosis	Team Effectiveness	Skills Building	Conflict Role	Problem Solving	Decision Making	Group Skills	Team Communication	Team Leadership
17	Communicating About Conflict	67						•				•	
18	Freeze Frame: Dealing with Problem Behaviours in Teams	71	•	•							•		
19	My Team and Me	73				•							
20	Mapping Team Success	77		•									
21	Darts: A Get Acquainted Activity	81	•										
22	Project "OP"	85			•			•		•			
23	The Victory Tour	89											
24	Creating a Team Mission	95										•	•
25	The Product Development Team	99										•	•
26	Transition Team Building	105			•	•							
27	Forming New Teams	107			•							•	
28	Linking Team Problem Solving with Corporate Strategy	115					•						
29	Team Building Interview Guide	119		•									
30	Visioning a Vision	123							•				
31	A Prescription for Team Effectiveness	125		•		•							
32	The Team of Your Life	127				•							
33	I Think I Make a Contribution	129		•									•

INDEX TO ACTIVITIES (Continued)

No.	TITLE	Team Leadership	Team Communication	Group Skills	Decision Making	Problem Solving	Conflict Role	Skills Building	Team Effectiveness	Diagnosis	Evaluations	Ice Breakers	Page
34	Team on Team						•						133
35	Team Development: A Grid Perspective									•			137
36	Selecting a Problem Solution					•							141
37	Selecting a Team Problem					•							145
38	Project Rescue							•		•			149
39	Roadblocks: A Constraint Activity							•					153
40	The Quality Case: An Ethical Dilemma				•								159
41	Tough Jobs												163
42	Questions We Ask Ourselves		•								•		169
43	Team Conflict Mode							•					173
44	That's Me: A Get Acquainted Activity											•	177
45	The Effective Team Member: A Consensus Activity							•					181
46	Creating a Team Logo		•										187
47	I'm Gonna Sit Right Down and Write Myself a Letter							•			•		189
48	Interdependent Images		•								•		191
49	SOS: An OD Intervention									•	•		193
50	Improving Team Meetings			•					•				197

13

ACTIVITIES

Activity 1

TRICKY TALES: A CROSS-TEAM TEAM BUILDING APPROACH

Purpose

1. To learn the difference between competitive and collaborative team behaviour.

2. To learn the techniques of cross-team teamwork.

Group Size

A minimum of sixteen people.

Time

Two hours.

Physical Setting

A large room with four round or rectangular tables and chairs spread out around the room so that the teams can have some privacy.

Materials

1. Four envelopes containing 3" x 5" cards prepared according to the *Directions for Preparing the Tricky Tales*.

2. A copy of *Teamwork Guidelines* for each person.

3. A copy of *Observer Guidelines* for each observer.

Process

1. Form four teams of at least four people each. Designate the teams 1, 2, 3, and 4. Ask one person from each team to volunteer to be an observer. Brief the observer using the *Observer Guidelines*.

2. Review the *Teamwork Guidelines* with the total group. Distribute the envelopes to the four teams.

3. The facilitator makes it clear that the activity is not over until all four teams have all the clues to their tale and the correct answer to their title.

4. The facilitator will tell the teams when they have all the clues and if they have the correct answer to their tale.

5. When everyone is finished, the observers provide feedback to their team and lead a discussion on things that helped and hindered the process.

6. The facilitator leads a discussion on how teams can work effectively with other teams. The session concludes with a lecturette on cross-team teamwork.

Variations

1. The activity can be made competitive by changing the directions to indicate that the first team to obtain all their clues and answer the tale is the winner.

2. The facilitator can pull the observers into a circle in the centre of the room for a discussion of their observations and learning on cross-team teamwork.

3. The tales can be changed to problems that are related to the work of the teams.

4. See Activity 25, The Product Development Team, for a similar activity.

TRICKY TALES

The Car Crash

A Mr. Smith and his son were driving in a car. The car crashed. The father was killed instantly. The son was critically injured and rushed to the hospital. The surgeon took a look at him and said, "I can't operate on him. He is my son, Arthur." How do you explain this?

How 'Bout Them Apples

A grocer has some apples for sale. One customer buys one-half of all the apples plus a half an apple. A second customer takes one-half of the remaining apples plus a half an apple. The third customer purchases one-half of the quantity left plus a half an apple. The grocer is not completely sold out. None of the customers bought fractions of apples. All purchases were whole numbers of apples. How many apples did the grocer originally have?

The Loser is a Winner

Each of two people owns a horse. Each person insists that his/her horse is the slowest. They were going to have a race to settle the argument but neither person would trust the other would ride to the fullest without the slightest holding back of the horse. How can the slowest horse be definitely established?

Sox Fox

There are 12 white socks and 49 red socks all mixed up in a drawer. These are individual socks not pairs. All the socks are the same size and made of the same material so no distinction can be made by any of your senses. What is the *minimum* number of socks you must pull out of the drawer, with your eyes closed, to ensure one matching pair was among those chosen?

19

DIRECTIONS FOR PREPARING THE TRICKY TALES

Each clue is printed on a 3" x 5" card. The letter and the number are included to make sure the cards are distributed across the four groups. The letters/numbers also help the facilitator determine if the team has all of the clues for their tale. All cards labelled "1" are placed in an envelope marked "1" and so on for the remaining three sets of cards. You should have four envelopes marked 1, 2, 3, and 4.

Tale 1

4	55	Mr. Smith and his son are driving in a car.
3	60	The car crashed.
1	65	The father was killed instantly.
2	70	The son was critically injured and rushed to the hospital.
1	75	The surgeon took a look at him and said, "I can't operate on him. He is my son, Arthur."
2	80	How do you explain this?

Tale 2

1	85	A grocer has some apples for sale.
3	90	One customer buys one-half of all the apples plus a half an apple.
3	95	A second customer takes one-half of the remaining apples plus a half an apple.
2	100	The third customer purchases one half of the quantity left plus a half an apple.
1	105	The grocer is now completely sold out.
3	110	None of the customers bought fractions of apples.
2	115	All purchases were whole numbers of apples.
1	120	How many apples did the grocer originally have?

Table 3

1	125	Each of two people own a horse.
2	130	Each person insists that his/her horse is the slowest.
3	135	They were going to have a race to settle the argument but neither person would trust that the other would ride to the fullest without the slightest holding back of the horse.
1	140	How can the slowest horse be definitely established?

Tale 4

2	145	There are 12 white socks and 49 red socks all mixed up in a drawer.
3	150	These are individual socks, not pairs.
1	155	All socks are the same size and made of the same material so no distinction can be made by any of the senses.
4	160	What is the *minimum* number of socks you must pull out of the drawer, with your eyes closed, to ensure one matching pair was among those chosen?

TEAMWORK GUIDELINES

Task
The team is to solve the tale. To accomplish this task each team must do two things: (1) obtain *all* clues and (2) determine the correct solution. The solution may not be submitted until all of the clues of the tale are in the team's possession. The facilitator will tell you if you have all the clues and your answer is correct.

Procedure
To obtain all the clues you negotiate with the other three teams for the clues. The rules for negotiation are:
1. Only one member of a team may leave the team at any one time.
2. Only one member may negotiate with any team at any one time.
3. Each member of the team must have at least one opportunity to negotiate with another team.
4. No more than two clues may be exchanged during any transaction with another team.

ANSWER KEY

1. The Car Crash:
The surgeon was Arthur's mother.

2. How 'Bout Them Apples:
The grocer originally had seven apples.

3. The Loser is the Winner:
Each person rides the other person's horse in a race.

4. Sox Fox:
If you take three socks from the drawer, two of the three must match since only two colours exist.

OBSERVER GUIDELINES

1 Sit where you can see and hear most of the team.

2. Take notes—include quotes where possible. Note the things that *help* and *hinder* the team and the *impact* of what was said or done.

3. Look for data on:

- COMPETITIVE BEHAVIOUR (working against the other teams)

- COLLABORATIVE BEHAVIOUR (working with the other teams)

- TASK ORIENTED BEHAVIOUR (keeping focused on the job to be done)

- STRATEGIC BEHAVIOUR (seeing the picture)

- PROCESS BEHAVIOUR (how the team is working together)

24

- CHALLENGING BEHAVIOUR (effectively disagreeing with others)

- NON-VERBAL BEHAVIOUR (communicating without words)

- DYSFUNCTIONAL BEHAVIOUR (e.g., side conversation, monopolizing)

- COMMENTS

Activity 2
YEA TEAM!

Purpose

1. To open a team training workshop with an energizing activity.
2. To help participants who are unfamiliar with each other to get acquainted.

Group Size

A minimum of twenty people is required. There is no maximum number. The activity can be done with a smaller group if the number of boxes on the grid is reduced.

Time

Forty-five minutes.

Physical Setting

A large room or section of a room that allows the participants to move easily around.

Materials

1. A copy of the *Team Grid* for each person.
2. Pencils or pens for each person.

Process

1. Explain the purpose of the activity. Distribute a copy of the *Team Grid*.
2. Explain the guidelines. The leader calls out items about people in the group and the participants write the items in boxes on the *Grid*. A few boxes may be designated as Wild Cards. Each box should have an item in it. See Activity 21, Darts: A Get Acquainted Activity, for a list of possible items.

3. Participants walk around the room and find people who are or can do the items in the boxes. When they find someone who fits the description, they ask the person to sign or initial the box. Participants try to get as many boxes signed as possible in the time available. Wild cards may be signed by anyone. However, a person may only sign one box on your grid, even though several items may apply to them. Time limit: 20 minutes.

4. The group reassembles. The leader explains that the goal is to spell *TEAM*. The first person to spell TEAM is the winner. The leader says "Put 'T' in box no. __. You may put a T in that box only if you have a signature in the box." The leader continues calling out 'E' in box no. __, 'A' in box no. __, 'M' in box no. __ until someone in the group can spell TEAM on their Grid. The person yells out "Yea Team!" and is declared the winner. You may continue to play until there are three winners.

5. We suggest small prizes for the winners such as T-shirts, sweatshirts, or hats.

Variations

1. Tailor the items for the boxes to the people in the group.

2. If the group is small, ask people to introduce themselves incorporating the items from the grid, after the activity.

3. Create small teams using items from the *Grid*. For example, all people who like to ski move to a corner of the room to discuss their interests. Then move on to related team issues.

1	2	3	4	5
6	7	8	9	10
11	12	13	14	15
16	17	18	19	20
21	22	23	24	25

Activity 3
GETTING TO KNOW THE BOSS

Purpose

1. To allow an intact work team to quickly become familiar with a new team leader.
2. To allow a new team leader to lay a foundation for team effectiveness.
3. To demonstrate the importance of open communication.

Time

Ninety minutes.

Group Size

An intact team of up to fifteen members.

Materials

Easel, flip chart pad, markers and Sellotape or drawing pins.

Physical Setting

A room large enough for the group to work comfortably with chairs in a circle or with a table and chairs arranged in a semicircular style.

Process

1. The new team leader begins by telling the work team that he/she would like to get to know the members quickly and open communication lines. The team leader explains the agenda, introduces the facilitator and leaves the meeting.
2. The facilitator gives a brief talk about the assimilation curve of new team leaders and the need for open communication.

3. Each participant is asked to pose a question he/she would like answered by the new leader.

   For example:

   • What are your measures of success?

   • How do you like to work?

   • What will get us in trouble with you?

The facilitator posts their questions and continues until everyone has had a chance to get their questions on the list.

4. The facilitator reviews and clarifies the list of questions.

5. The new team leader returns to the meeting and, guided by the facilitator, the new leader answers each question.

6. The team leader then agrees to hold ongoing sessions to keep communication lines open. Frequency, duration and location of meetings are decided.

8. The facilitator summarizes the meeting.

Variations

1. The team leader acts as facilitator.

2. Members can be asked to prepare their questions in advance of the meeting.

3. Additional questions can be asked by members after the team leader finishes in step 6.

4. For a related activity, see Activity 26, Transition Team Building.

Activity 4
ROBIN HOOD—AN EMPOWERMENT ACTIVITY

Purpose

1. To help team members identify those things they can do to help them be more effective.
2. To make the group aware of the concept of work team self-direction.
3. To assist the leader in empowering their team.

Group Size

A maximum of eight members of an intact team.

Time

Two hours.

Physical Setting

A room large enough for the team to be comfortable and wall space for posting flip chart pages.

Chairs can be arranged in a circle or a table and chairs can be arranged in seminar style.

Materials

Easel, flip charts, markers, and Sellotape or drawing pins.

Process

1. The team leader begins by telling the group of his/her commitments to empowering the team and introduces the facilitator. The team leader then leaves the group.

2. The facilitator gives a brief lecturette on the motion of empowering work teams so that they can be more effective in their tasks.

3. The facilitator then asks the team members to generate a list of ways they can be involved in the decision making process of the team.

4. The team clarifies the list and narrows the list to the top three actions they would like to see taken.

5. The team then prepares an action plan for the top three actions.

6. The team leader returns and the group presents their work and negotiates the action plans with the team leader.

7. The facilitator summarizes and processes the meeting. The team leader sets a date and time for a follow-up review.

Variations

1. The team leader can stay for the entire meeting.

2. If the team has difficulty determining the three action items, they can vote on the list. One way to "vote" is to give each team member ten votes which can be distributed among the items on the list. In other words, they can give one item all ten votes or give one vote to ten different items.

Activity 5
THE BALL GAME

Purpose

1. To reinforce the concept of continuous improvement.
2. To reinforce problem-solving techniques.
3. To close a team building or training session on a positive note.

Group Size

Works best with a team or training group of five to fifteen people.

Time

Thirty minutes.

Physical Setting

A room or a section of a large room with no tables and chairs. This activity can also be done outside.

Materials

A small, soft ball that is easy to throw and catch.

Process

1. Explain that the team is going to learn together by playing a ball game.

2. The team stands and forms a circle with nothing in the centre. The leader throws the ball to one person and instructs the person to give the ball to another person and call his or her name. The game continues until each person has been given the ball. All members of the team are told to remember the name of the person to whom they gave the ball. After the team finishes, the leader asks, "Can you do it better and faster?" The team usually moves the circle in closer and runs through it again. When they finish, the leader asks, "Can you do it better and faster?" The team usually moves in closer and runs through it again. The process continues until the team is satisfied that they have done their best. By this time, they are usually standing next each other in a tight circle.

3. The leader concludes the session by summarizing learning on problem-solving and continuous quality improvement.

Activity 6
REALLY ... BUT I THOUGHT!

Purpose

1. To clarify expectations and conceptions of team members.
2. To renegotiate roles within/among a work team.
3. To create awareness of the need for personal contracting.

Group Size

A minimum of twelve members of an intact team.

Time

Two hours.

Physical Setting

A large room with wall space for posting flip chart pages, chairs in a circle or around a conference table.

Materials

1. Easel, flip chart, markers and Sellotape or drawing pins.
2. Personal pads for all team members.

Process

1. The team leader or facilitator gives a brief presentation on the four characteristics of role as defined by Gordon Allport:

   - Role Expectations — What others expect of us
   - Role Conception — What you see your role to be
   - Role Acceptance — How we accept our role
   - Role Behaviour — How we actually behave

37

2. The facilitator asks each member to work privately and evaluate the other members (including themselves) on the four elements (30 minutes).

3. The facilitator then asks the members to pair off randomly and share their work with each team member. This activity should continue until each team member has had a one-on-one meeting with every other team member.

4. The facilitator gives a brief presentation on personal contracting and asks each team member to make a new contract with each team member.

5. The team concludes the activity by setting a time and date to review progress.

Variations

1. Step 2 can be done as pre-work.

2. The private negotiating sessions can be done in a group forum.

Activity 7
DEALING WITH PROBLEM PEOPLE ON TEAMS

Purpose

1. To identify the types of behaviour that interfere with effective team meetings.
2. To develop specific techniques for dealing with problem people on your team.

Group Size

Since this activity is designed for a team training workshop, the size of the group is limited only by the space available and the ability of the leader to handle large groups; works best with a group of up to twenty.

Time

One to one and a half hours.

Physical Setting

Table and chairs in seminar style or a U-shape.

Materials

A copy of *Handling Problems in Team Meetings* for each person.

Process

1. Explain the purpose of the activity and distribute the handout. Ask each person to complete the exercise alone.
2. Ask for volunteers to indicate how they would handle each type of behaviour. Probe for specific words or actions. Paraphrase their responses to let them hear how it sounds.

3. Conclude the session by presenting a list of interventions for dealing with dysfunctional behaviour in groups (e.g., listen, set/enforce norms, negotiate, confront).

Variations

1. Form sub-teams and assign one or two behaviours to each team to discuss and develop interventions.

2. Simulate a team meeting and ask participants to role play several of the behaviours. Other team members are asked to respond to the problem behaviour during the simulation.

3. A related activity is Activity 18, Freeze Frame: Dealing with Problem Behaviours in Teams.

HANDLING PROBLEMS IN TEAM MEETINGS

PROBLEM BEHAVIOURS   **WHAT WOULD YOU
                                            SAY OR DO?**

1. Silence—member does not participate.   _____

2. Overly long comment.   _____

3. Too much humour or wisecracking.   _____

4. Consistently arrives late.   _____

5. Consistently leaves before the meeting _____
    is over.

6. Sidetracking (comments are way   _____
    off subject).

7. Rushes team to a quick decision or
    to end meeting too fast.   _____

8. Engages in side conversations.   _____

9. Monopolizes the discussion.   _____

10. Introduces personal problem or
    concern.   _____

Activity 8

RESOLVING INTERGROUP CONFLICT

Purpose

1. To help two teams identify the sources of their conflict.
2. To help two teams develop a plan for resolving their conflict.

Group Size

A team building session for two teams. Works best with teams of no more than ten people each.

Time

One day.

Physical Setting

One large meeting room and one small break-out room.

Materials

Easel, flip chart, Sellotape or drawing pins.

Process

1. Explain the purpose of the activity. Set some positive norms for the session (e.g., listening, focusing on the issue).
2. Ask one group to move to the break-out room while the other one stays in the meeting room. Each team is to prepare a list of answers to these two questions:

- What does the other team do that inhibits our ability to get our job done or, in general, just "bugs" us?
- What do we do that inhibits the other team's ability to get its job done or in general "bugs" them?

3. The teams reassemble in the large room and post their flip charts on the wall. Team members walk around and read the lists.

4. Team members are encouraged to ask questions for clarification of the items on the lists.

5. The facilitator leads a discussion directed toward the identification of key issues standing in the way of effective intergroup teamwork. The most important issues are listed on the flip chart. If too many issues are listed, they should be ranked in order of importance.

6. The facilitator writes each issue on a separate sheet of flip chart and posts them on the wall around the room. Participants may work on the issue that interests them by moving to the area where the flip chart paper is posted. Teams are formed on this basis to develop action plans for addressing the issue. The only stipulations are that the teams include a reasonably equal number of people from each group and that the team not be too large.

7. Teams are asked to come up with a problem statement, causes of the problem and an action plan, including responsibilities and a timetable. Each team prepares and presents a report on its plans. The other teams react.

9. The session concludes with a summary by the facilitator and a review of next steps based on the action plans.

Variations

1. The facilitator meets with each team prior to the session and collects data on the relationships using the same questions. The session begins with a summary of the comments.

2. See Activity 9, A Breath of Fresh Air, for another intergroup activity.

Activity 9
A BREATH OF FRESH AIR

Purpose

1. To air issues and problems between two work teams.
2. To improve inter-team relations.

Time

Three hours.

Group Size

Two teams of ten or more.

Materials

Easel, flip charts and markers for each team.

Physical Setting

A large room for the general session and one break-out room.

Process

1. The facilitator gives a briefing on the process of the meeting and a talk on the need for quality inter-team relationships (10–15 min.).
2. The facilitator tells the teams to meet separately and record answers to the following questions.
   - How would the other team characterize our team?
   - How would we characterize them?
3. The teams complete the task.
4. The teams reassemble and present their lists. The facilitator gives a short briefing on reacting to the lists and tells the group that the only reaction that's okay is questioning for clarification (10 min.).

5. The teams begin by having a reporter read the answers to each question (20 min.).

6. The process is repeated for the second group (20 min.).

7. The answer sheets are exchanged and the teams are directed to return to their separate work areas and formulate responses to both lists (30 min.).

8. The teams reassemble and present their responses (30 min.).

9. The teams discuss responses and break up into sub-teams to refine responses and gather more data about the issues.

10. The teams reassemble and using the new data answer the following question:

    • How can we develop a solid working relationship with the other team? (30 min.).

11. The large group reassembles and each team presents its work (15 min.).

12. The facilitator wraps-up by leading a discussion on the benefit of a good working relationship between teams. The facilitator then gives a lecturette on follow up and assessing the success of the effort.

13. The facilitator leads a discussion on the process of the meeting.

Variations

1. The initial questions can be changed from image questions to task questions, such as:

    • What do we need from the other team to achieve our goals?

    • What do we owe the other team so they can achieve their goals?

2. See Activity 8, Resolving Intergroup Conflict, for a related exercise.

Activity 10

SELF-RENEWAL: AN ACTIVITY FOR A MATURE TEAM

Purpose

1. To help a mature team engage in self examination.
2. To provide a mature team with a process for renewal.

Group Size

A team building activity that works best with an intact team of four to eight people.

Time

Three hours.

Physical Setting

A small room with chairs arranged in a circle or around a small conference table.

Materials

Easel, flip chart, markers, and Sellotape or drawing pins.

Process

1. Prior to the session each person should prepare answers to two questions about the team:
   - Things we should preserve.
   - Things we should change.
2. The responses should be posted on flip charts.

3. At the beginning of the session team members walk around the room and read the charts.

4. The team identifies the key things they should preserve and discusses ways to enhance these strengths in the future. They develop action times as appropriate.

5. The team identifies the most important things they need to change and discusses ways to implement these changes. They develop action items as appropriate.

6. The session closes with a summary of the results and next steps. The team discusses their feelings about the renewal process.

Variations

1. Eliminate the pre-work. Begin the session with brainstorming the answers to the two questions.

2. If many things are identified as important, create sub-teams to work on each area.

Activity 11
THE CAR CASE

Purpose

1. To teach quality and other problem-solving teams how to recognize a real problem.
2. To teach quality and other problem-solving teams how to write a clear problem statement.

Group Size

Works with an intact team of up to twelve people or as a session in team training workshop. In a training workshop, the class can be divided into small groups with each one doing this activity.

Time

Forty-five minutes to one hour.

Physical Setting

Round or rectangular table and chairs.

Materials

1. A copy *The Car Case* for each person.
2. Easel, flip chart, markers, Sellotape or drawing pins or overhead projector, screen and transparency pens.

Process

1. Explain the purpose of the session. Ask teams to brainstorm answers to the question, "What is a Problem?" Post answers on flip charts or overhead transparency.
2. Distribute *The Car Case*. Ask the team to read the case, decide what they think is the problem and write a problem statement.

3. The facilitator leads a discussion on the team answers and writes the problem statement developed by the team on the flip chart or overhead transparency. The statement is edited by the team.

4. The session concludes with a lecturette on problems and problem statements. The original brainstormed list is used as a springboard for the lecturette.

Variations

1. Present the lecturette on what is a problem and the elements of a good problem statement prior to analysing the case.

2. Prior to working on the case give the team some sample problem statements to analyse to determine if they meet the criteria of an acceptable problem statement.

3. A related activity is Activity 37, Selecting a Team Problem.

THE CAR CASE

Background Information: Your job requires you to be at work promptly at 7:00 a.m. to relieve the midnight shift operator. You live 20 minutes from the job, driving by car.

Your wife/husband also works and has a car which he/she uses to take the kids two miles to school on his/her way to work. They start school at 8:00 a.m., and he/she begins work at 8:30 a.m. One of your children has a driver's licence.

You have a neighbour two houses away who works where you do but he begins work at 7:30 a.m., 30 minutes later than you do. He carpools with two other men.

There is a bus that passes a block away from your house and goes by the plant. However, the first bus in the morning does not get to the plant until 7:30 a.m.

THE SITUATION

On Monday morning, you go to the car as usual at 6:35 a.m. and find that it will not start. It will turn over slowly but will not start. You not only need the car to get to work but you need it to go out of town to a training session tomorrow morning. This is the third time this winter the car has not started.

What is the problem?

Write a problem statement.

51

Activity 12
WHY ARE WE HERE?

Purpose

1. To create an agenda for a team meeting.
2. To identify a set of commonly perceived issues facing a work team.
3. To develop team effectiveness skills.

Group Size

This exercise works best with an intact team of twelve or less.

Time

One hour.

Physical Setting

A room large enough for the team to work comfortably, with wall space for posting flip chart paper.

Materials

Easel, flip chart, markers, or drawing pins.

Process

1. The facilitator discusses the goals of the activity and gives an overview of the process.
2. Team members are asked to form triads and answer the following question:
   * What issues should we deal with during this meeting?
3. Each triad posts their answers on a flip chart, then reassembles and present their lists.

4. Lists are posted on a wall. Duplicate issues are eliminated. Similar items are combined.

5. Each triad then selects the three most important issues.

6. The facilitator prepares a new list of all the important issues.

7. The facilitator asks the participants to rank order the new list according to the urgency of the issue. The most urgent issue should be ranked "1" and so on.

8. The facilitator tallies the rankings.

9. The final rank order list of the issues is posted.

Variations

1. A criterion other than "urgency" can be used. For example:

   * issues that we control, or
   * issues that we can resolve today

2. Team members can be asked to submit their issues to the leader prior to the meeting. The meeting starts with a presentation of the list of all issues submitted. The team discusses the issues and ranks them.

3. Another way to create an agenda is to use a team assessment survey. See Activity 15, Characteristics of an Effective Work Team: An Assessment Activity.

Activity 13
SKILLS FOR SALE

Purpose

1. To critically review the skills, capabilities and potential of a team.

2. To develop a strategy for marketing the services of a team.

3. To explore a team's strengths and weaknesses.

Group Size

This is a team building activity designed for use with an intact work team of up to twelve people.

Time

Three hours.

Physical Setting

Chairs arranged in a circle or tables and chairs arranged in conference style.

Materials

1. Easel, flip charts, markers, Sellotape or drawing pins.

2. Paper and pens for each team member.

Process

1. The team leader tells the group that they are to imagine that they are an internal consulting group (consulting in the general area of their unit's expertise) in a large industrial organization. Further, they are told that because the economy isn't doing well changes in the business will have to be made. In fact, the team leader's boss has made it clear that the group will have to become a profit centre by marketing its services to the outside world and earn more than half its budget. The alternative is to shut down the department and lay-off the staff.

   The team leader is given six months to launch the new unit.

2. The team leader then leads the group through an identification of their skills and capabilities and determination as to which skills might be marketable.

3. The team identifies its shortcomings and any additional skills that will be needed.

4. The team determines how the current skills can be enhanced and additional skills can be acquired.

5. The team leader then reviews what has been learned during the activity and lists action steps to be taken.

6. At the end of the session the team leader and the members process the activity and build an action plan to implement the steps needed to enhance the team's overall skill base.

Variations

1. The skills assessment activity can be done in advance.

2. The team can obtain input from their current customers based on their skills and capabilities. The input can also include ideas on what additional skills and capabilities the customers would like to see the team develop.

Activity 14
TMS—A PROCESS FOR ROLE CLARIFICATION

Purpose

1. To clarify the roles played in a team.
2. To clarify expectations held of other members and themselves.
3. To understand the process of role adjustment.

Group Size

No more than twelve members of an intact team.

Time

Two hours.

Physical Setting

A private room with wall space for posting flip charts.

Materials

1. Easel, flip chart, markers and Sellotape or drawing pins.
2. Copies of the *TMS Questionnaire*.
3. Paper and pen for team members.

Process

1. The facilitator presents a lecture on the three elements of TMS Model: Task Oriented Roles, Maintenance-Oriented Roles and Self-Oriented Roles.
2. The facilitator asks the members to complete the TMS questionnaire on themselves only.

3. The facilitator asks the group for a volunteer.

4. The facilitator asks the members to complete a TMS questionnaire on the volunteer.

5. The volunteer then tells team members what he/she thinks the other members of the team have said about him/her.

6. The volunteer then questions the other team members and records their actual response.

7. The facilitator leads a discussion of the responses.

8. The volunteer and team members engage in a discussion of the results guided by the facilitator.

9. The facilitator conducts a renegotiation resulting in a new contract between the volunteer and fellow team members.

10. Steps 3-9 are repeated until all team members have a chance to participate.

Variations

1. Each team member can complete the TMS questionnaire on themselves and the other team members prior to the meeting.

2. Another individual assessment activity is Activity 33, I Think I Make a Contribution

TMS QUESTIONNAIRE

Task-Oriented Roles • Maintenance-Oriented Roles • Self-Oriented Roles

Task-Oriented Roles: Contribute to the ability of the group to accomplish its objective.

		Low				High
1.	Initiating Interaction	1	2	3	4	5
2.	Giving/Seeking Information	1	2	3	4	5
3.	Giving/Seeking Opinions	1	2	3	4	5
4.	Clarifying	1	2	3	4	5
5.	Summarizing	1	2	3	4	5

Maintenance Roles: Contribute to the ability of the team to create and maintain effective interpersonal relations.

1.	Harmonizing	1	2	3	4	5
2.	Compromising	1	2	3	4	5
3	Supporting	1	2	3	4	5
4.	Gatekeeping	1	2	3	4	5
5.	Encouraging	1	2	3	4	5

Self-Oriented Roles: Do not contribute to the effectiveness of the team.

1.	Blocking	1	2	3	4	5
2.	Withdrawing	1	2	3	4	5
3.	Dominating	1	2	3	4	5
4.	Being Aggressive	1	2	3	4	5
5.	Criticizing	1	2	3	4	5

Activity 15
CHARACTERISTICS OF AN EFFECTIVE WORK TEAM: AN ASSESSMENT ACTIVITY

Purpose

1. To assess the effectiveness of a team.
2. To plan for the improvement of a team.

Group Size

Works best with an intact team with less than twenty people.

Time   Two hours.

Physical Setting

Chairs arranged in a circle or tables arranged in a U- shape.

Materials

A copy of *Characteristics of an Effective Work Team* for each person.

Process

1. Prior to the meeting the survey should be completed by each person. The facilitator should summarize the results and prepare a report for the team.
2. At the meeting, present the summary, and ask the team to identify key strengths and improvement opportunities. Strengths are high in description and importance. Improvement opportunities are low in description and high in importance.

61

3. Isolate up to three key areas the team would like to address. If the team is small, the whole team can develop action plans for each area. With a large team, sub-teams can be formed, with each sub-team asked to work on one of the areas.

4. The session concludes with plans and action steps for each area.

5. The team should plan to periodically revisit the area to monitor progress.

Variations

1. Complete the survey in class and summarize the results on the flip chart.

2. Tailor the survey to reflect current issues on the team.

3. Another approach is to interview team members. See Activity 29, Team Building Interview Guide.

CHARACTERISTICS OF AN EFFECTIVE WORK TEAM

Please circle the number that indicates the degree to which you feel the following characteristics are descriptive of your team, and the number that indicates the degree to which you feel each characteristic is important to the functioning of the team.

	DESCRIPTION					IMPORTANCE				
	NEVER	SELDOM	SOMETIMES	USUALLY	ALWAYS	UNIMPORTANT	SOMEWHAT IMPORTANT	IMPORTANT	VERY IMPORTANT	CRITICAL
1. *Clear Task:* The task or objective of the group is well understood and accepted by the group.	1	2	3	4	5	1	2	3	4	5
2. *Informality:* The "atmosphere" tends to be informal, comfortable, relaxed. There are no obvious tensions or signs of boredom.	1	2	3	4	5	1	2	3	4	5
3. *Participation:* There is a lot of discussion in which virtually everyone participates, but it remains pertinent to the task of the group.	1	2	3	4	5	1	2	3	4	5
4. *Listening:* The members listen to each other! Every idea is given a hearing.	1	2	3	4	5	1	2	3	4	5
5, *Disagreement:* There is disagreement but the team is comfortable with this and shows no signs of avoiding conflict to keep everything on a plane of sweetness and light.	1	2	3	4	5	1	2	3	4	5
6. *Consensus:* Most decisions are reached by consensus; formal voting is kept to a minimum.	1	2	3	4	5	1	2	3	4	5
7. *Open Communications:* Team members feel free to express their feelings on the task as well as the group's operation. There is little "pussyfooting" and few hidden agendas.	1	2	3	4	5	1	2	3	4	5
8. *Clear Assignment:* When action is taken, clear assignments are made and accepted.	1	2	3	4	5	1	2	3	4	5
9. *Shared Leadership:* While the team has a formal leader, leadership functions shift from time to time depending upon the circumstances, the needs of the group and the skills of the members.	1	2	3	4	5	1	2	3	4	5
10. *Self-Assessment:* Periodically, the team stops to examine how well it is functioning and what may be interfering with its effectiveness.	1	2	3	4	5	1	2	3	4	5

Activity 16
DRAWINGS

Purpose

1. To assess the current state of collaboration among teams in an organization.

2. To improve collaboration among teams in an organization.

Group Size

Five to forty people in a team building session.

Time

Two hours.

Physical Setting

A large room with a round or rectangular table, and chairs for each team.

Materials

A set of the following materials for each team:

1. Book of drawing paper
2. Coloured pens
3. Transparent Sellotape
4. Blank paper

Process

1. Explain that the purpose of the activity is to create a book of cartoons that reflects the current state of collaboration among teams in the organization. Teams may only use the materials provided. One book is to be prepared which is the combined efforts of all teams. Each team may only send one person at any time to another team to communicate about the project. There is a time limit of one hour.

65

2. At the conclusion of the activity, the cartoons should be shared and discussed as a basis for identifying cross-team collaboration problems. The discussion should also bring out what was learned from working together on this project.

3. The facilitator should help the group come up with action ideas to address the problems.

4. The session should conclude with a lecturette on the obstacles and strategies for effective inter-team collaboration.

Variations

1. After problems have been identified, ask each team to analyse one of the problems and devise an action plan for it.

2. For related activities, see Activity 8, Resolving Intergroup Conflict and Activity 9, A Breath of Fresh Air.

Activity 17
COMMUNICATING ABOUT CONFLICT

Purpose

1. To share approaches to dealing with conflict in a team setting.
2. To learn alternative approaches to dealing with conflict.

Group Size

Four to twelve people is preferred. This exercise is most appropriate for team building but it may be adapted for use in team training workshops. In a workshop, a larger group may be divided into several small teams for the purpose of this activity.

Time

One to two hours.

Physical Setting

For team building, arrange chairs in a circle; for training, arrange several groups of chairs in a circle or use a round table and chairs.

Materials

Copies of *Communicating About Conflict*.

Process

1. Explain the purpose of the exercise. Distribute the handout.
2. Ask for a volunteer to begin with the first question. Follow the directions on the handout.
3. The facilitator should probe for clarification, elaboration and for appropriate interventions.

4. Summarize key learning about conflict and what changes in the team are necessary in order to facilitate effective conflict resolution.

5. Conclude the session with a lecturette on conflict styles and their advantages and disadvantages.

Variations

1. Change the questions and statements to more closely fit the issues on your team.

2.. The facilitator and/or team members can demonstrate how different conflict styles would react to the various questions and comments.

3. The session can conclude with each person discussing how they plan to handle conflict differently in the future.

4. For an exercise focusing on how a team deals with conflict, see Activity 43, Team Conflict Mode.

COMMUNICATING ABOUT CONFLICT

Directions: The list of open-ended statements below is designed to stimulate group discussion. You are not limited to the ones on this list. The following ground rules apply.

- Take turns initiating the discussion by completing a statement or asking someone else on the team to complete a statement.

- You must be willing to complete any statement that you ask someone else to complete.

- Any member may decline to complete any statement that someone else initiates.

- All discussion remains confidential.

Statements may be taken in any order:

1. Conflict is . . .
2. The time I felt best about dealing with conflict was . . .
3. When things are not going well I tend to . . .
4. I sometimes avoid unpleasant situations by . . .
5. When someone disagrees with me about something important I usually . . .
6. When someone challenges me in front of others I usually . . .
7. I feel most vulnerable during a conflict when . . .
8. On this team we usually handle conflict by . . .
9. I usually hide or camouflage my feelings when . . .
10. When I get angry I . . .
11. When someone avoids conflict with me I . . .
12. I am most likely to assert myself in situations that . . .
13. My greatest strength in handling conflict is . . .
14. In this team I would have the most difficulty with . . .
15. The most important outcome of conflict is . . .

Activity 18

FREEZE FRAME: DEALING WITH PROBLEM BEHAVIOURS IN TEAMS

Purpose

1. To identify and describe behaviours that interfere with team effectiveness.
2. To develop a set of interventions that minimize or eliminate the behaviours.

Group Size

Fifteen to forty people in a team training workshop.

Time

Two-and-a-half hours.

Physical Setting

A room large enough for groups of five to eight people to work without overhearing each other.

Movable chairs; no tables.

Materials

Easel, flip chart, markers and drawing pins.

Process

1. Facilitator outlines the goals of the session and explains that the participants' actual experiences with problem behaviours will be used as data for learning rather than hypothetical cases.
2. Facilitator asks the participants to briefly describe behaviours they have observed in groups that were counter-productive and/or difficult for them to handle (e.g., monopolizing, excessive wisecracking, attacking the leader or the agenda). Brief one-line summaries of these behaviours are posted on the flip chart. No more than eight or ten behaviours should be listed.

3. Using the consensus method reduce the list to no less than three or more than six behaviours depending upon the size of the group. The two main criteria for reducing the list are: (1) behaviours that produce the most difficulty and (2) behaviours that occur most frequently.

4. Facilitator writes an abbreviated version of the behaviours on a sheet of flip chart paper — one behaviour per sheet. The sheets are posted in different corners or sections of the room.

5. Facilitator explains that each person should select the behaviour on which he/she wants to work and move to the section of the room where the flip chart paper describing the behaviour is posted. The groups that have now been formed complete the following task:

   a. Discuss their experiences with the behaviour and how they have handled the person.

   b. Prepare a vignette, of no more than two minutes, which depicts the behaviour with members of the group acting as:

      (1) Narrator — sets the stage for the vignette by explaining who, when, where, etc.

      (2) Facilitator — serves as leader in the vignette and afterwards pulls and processes the learning.

      (3) Group members — problem behaviour participants and others as required to simulate the event.

   c. Present the vignette up to the point where the behaviour occurs but before the facilitator intervenes. The frame freezes at this point.

6. Each group presents its vignette and stops when the behaviour has been depicted. The facilitator in the group then asks participants from other groups to indicate how they would intervene at this point.

7. Several of the proposed interventions are tried by the facilitator with the group. All ideas are posted on the flip chart. The group also presents at least one of their interventions.

8. This format continues until all groups have presented their vignette.

9. Facilitator concludes the session by identifying the interventions that are generally applicable to all situations and presenting his/her ideas for handling problems.

Variations

1. For a less complex activity, see Activity 7, Dealing with Problem People on Teams.

Activity 19
MY TEAM AND ME

Purpose

To help a team identify those factors that affect the degree of positive identification with the team and its purpose.

Group Size

Unlimited. This activity is designed for use with an intact work team.

Time

One hour.

Physical Setting

A space large enough for the group to work comfortably and to be able to post their work for each member to view.

Materials

1. Copy of the *Team Identification Model (TIM)*.
2. Easel, flip charts, markers and Sellotape or drawing pins.

Process

1. The team leader hands out copies of the TIM instructions and blank TIM forms.
2. Members are asked to read the instructions sheet and complete the TIM form.
3. Once members have completed their TIM forms they post them on the wall and engage in a "walk around" to view the work of other members.
4. The team reassembles for a discussion that seeks to clarify and analyse the various responses.
5. With the leader, members develop ways to help increase identification with the team.

73

Variations

The team leader can compile the results of the members' work and report for the entire team.

TEAM IDENTIFICATION MODEL

Instructions: The *TIM Form* is composed of ten belief statements that reflect an individual team member's identification with the purpose and goals of the team. The level of strength of each belief can contribute to either enhancing or detracting from an individual team member's identification with the team's goals.

1. Review each of the ten belief statements below.
2. For each belief statement listed below, assign a strength value, one being a weak belief and five being a strong belief.

TIM STATEMENTS	BELIEF STRENGTH SCALE WEAK				STRONG
1. My belief in the team's overall purpose.	1	2	3	4	5
2. My belief in the team's ability to achieve its purpose.	1	2	3	4	5
3. My belief in the team's willingness to support fellow members.	1	2	3	4	5
4. My belief that the team is able to be self-directed and self-renewing.	1	2	3	4	5
5. My belief in the team development process.	1	2	3	4	5
6. My belief in the team's current working objectives.	1	2	3	4	5
7. My belief that the rest of the organization perceives the team positively.	1	2	3	4	5
8. My belief in the team's link to the wider organizational goals.	1	2	3	4	5
9. My belief that there is a clear match between the team's goals and my personal goals.	1	2	3	4	5
10. My belief in the leader's willingness to support the team members.	1	2	3	4	5

Activity 20
MAPPING TEAM SUCCESS

Purpose

1. To explore the past accomplishments and activities of a team.
2. To graph the successes and failures of a team.
3. To use the charts to plot a team's future.

Group Size

Unlimited. This activity is designed for use only with an intact work group.

Time

At least two hours of meeting time and at least one to two hours of pre-work.

Physical Setting

A space large enough to allow each team member to post his/her graphs so they may be viewed by all team members.

Materials

1. Chart paper and pens for each participant.
2. Masking tape or drawing pins to mount charts.
3. Flip chart paper and marking pens.
4. Copy of *Team Success Chart* for each person.

Process

1. The facilitator discusses with the group the Mapping Team Success process. By identifying the success a team has achieved over a defined period of time, a team is able to reach a consensus on the activities that lead to success and to ensure future success.

2. Each team member completes a *Team Success Chart*; this analysis is a reflection of each team member's personal perceptions of how successful the team has been and why. The *Team Success Chart* is composed of a time axis and a success axis. The time axis should be divided into time periods appropriate for the group. Success can be measured by months or quarters, for example, depending upon the success cycle of the group. The success axis is the individual team member's perceptions of the team's overall success. A score of "0" indicates no success, a score of "7' indicates 100% achievement.

3. Team members should post and display their *Team Success Charts*. After the team members have inspected each other's charts, the group should reassemble and discuss each other's scores and perceptions.

4. The facilitator should lead a problem-solving session to identify the methods for achieving success and the reasons for high or low success.

5. The team develops an action plan to increase the success of the team.

6. At a later date, the team reconvenes to follow up on their action plan and evaluates the changes that were implemented.

Variations

1. Team leader only completes the *Team Success Chart* as pre-work.

2. Task groups are assigned to work on specific problems to be solved.

3. Another team assessment activity is Activity 15, Characteristics of an Effective Work Team: An Assessment Activity.

TEAM SUCCESS CHART

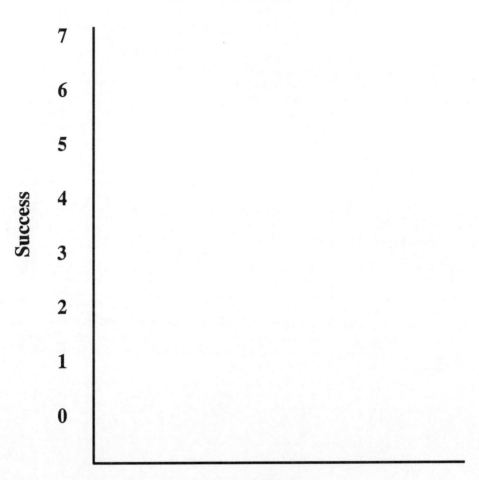

Activity 21
DARTS: A GET ACQUAINTED ACTIVITY

Purpose

1. To help workshop participants who are unfamiliar with each other to get to know each other at the beginning of the programme.
2. To set a positive, informal and relaxed learning climate.
3. To have fun!

Group Size

Twenty to two hundred people. The activity requires at least twenty people unless the dart board is altered to include fewer items.

Time

One hour.

Physical Setting

A large room with movable chairs.

Materials

1. A copy of the *Dart Board* for each person.
2. Three prizes for the winners. We suggest inexpensive but fun items such as a T-shirt, sweatshirt, or hat.

Process

1. Prior to the session come up with at least twenty items that are related to the group or are general enough to be applicable to any group. See the *Dart Board Ideas* for sample items.

2. Provide each person with the *Dart Board*. Explain the guidelines:
   - Write the items in any box.
   - After the Board has been completed, walk around and find people who are or can do the items in the boxes. Ask the person to sign that box.
   - A person can only sign one of your boxes.
3. Call out the items and have the people fill in their Board.
4. People walk around and get the signatures.
5. After about 15 minutes call "Time" and ask people to take their seats.
6. Call out the items in random order. Explain that if they have the box signed they are to write an "X" in the box. The first person to get 75 points wins. When a person gets 75 they are to yell "Bulls-eye!" Play the game until three people get 75.

Variations

1. If the group is 20–25 participants in size you can ask people to introduce themselves after the game is over. Their introduction should include aspects of the items applicable to them. For example, "My name is Glenn Parker, I am an only child; born in Highbury, I support Arsenal."

2. After the game is over, small groups can be formed around some of the items. For example, "all people who have travelled to the USA meet over in this corner of the room. Share with others where you went and what you liked about it."

3. The game can be continued by forming teams. For example, the first five people who get to 75 will be one team; the next five to get to 75 will be another team. When the teams meet they can introduce each other incorporating the items from the board.

4. A similar get acquainted activity is Activity 2, Yea Team!

DART BOARD IDEAS

Travelled to the USA in the last 12 months

An only child

Likes to ski

Collects antiques

Is a grandparent

Does volunteer work

Born outside the UK

Born in (county)

Knows the capital of Canada

Can name the seven dwarfs

Reads *Hello* magazine and will admit it

Has performed on stage

Been with the company less than a year (more than 20 years)

Been to a concert in the last three months

Plays golf

Knows someone famous

Owns a personal computer

Supports (sports team)

DART BOARD

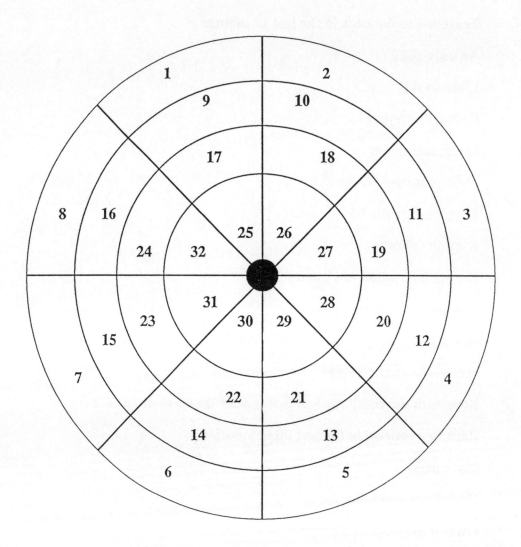

Activity 22
PROJECT "OP"

Purpose

1. To explore the dynamics of status, power and information in decision making.

2. To explore the impact of inter-team perceptions on team effectiveness.

3. To assess contributions to overall team effectiveness.

Group Size

Unlimited (in non-intact teams) number of teams can be formed of five to seven members.

Time

Two to three hours.

Physical Setting

Chairs arranged in a circle or a round or rectangular table with chairs for each team. Room should be large enough for each team to have a private discussion.

Materials

1. One copy of *Project "OP" Information Sheet* for each participant.

2. Flip chart, marker, Sellotape or drawing pins for each team.

Process

1. The facilitator begins by giving a short talk on the dynamics of status, power and information as they relate to decision making.

2. A general discussion is held regarding the impact that perception has on team effectiveness.

3. Groups are formed and given the *Instruction Sheet*. The team members are given a few minutes to acquaint themselves with the material and then begin the activity.

85

4. After 90 minutes the facilitator concludes the session and reconvenes the large group.

5. Each group presents a summary of their work as follows:

    a.   Describe how you began.

    b.   Discuss how information was used to influence the decision making process.

    c.   Discuss the general tenor of your session.

    d.   Discuss the final result.

6. The session is concluded by the facilitator with a general discussion of power and influence in teams and how to manage it.

PROJECT "OP" INFORMATION SHEET

The Problem: How are the limited number of work days to be distributed among the team members?

The Background: You are all employed by DEI, Inc., a consulting firm specializing in outplacement and job development services.

A project called "OP" has been awarded to DEI and, in turn, to your group. Your total group is composed of 20 consultants all of whom work as independents (i.e., you get paid daily rates only when you actually perform services).

Some members of your team have worked for DEI before and may have access to scheduling assignment data from other projects.

THE TEAM TASK

The purpose of this meeting of 5–7 members is to determine an equitable way to divide the days available for Project "OP" among the total group of 20, as well as the bonus money that will be available if the project goes well.

The exact number of days of work available is not yet determined but is rumoured to be about the same as in the past projects.

Your group task is to find an equitable system for dividing the number of days available for the project among all members of the team.

Activity 23
THE VICTORY TOUR

Purpose

1. To demonstrate the need for team goals.

2. To demonstrate team meeting management skills.

3. To experience the impact of personal agendas on team effectiveness.

Group Size

Designed for a team training workshop. The group is divided into teams of six people. The number of teams is limited only by the space available and the ability of the facilitator to handle large groups.

Time

Two to three hours.

Physical Setting

A table and chairs for each team in a room large enough so that the teams can work without hearing each other.

Materials

1. *Leader's Instruction Sheet* for each team leader.

2. *Observation Guide.*

3. *Data Sheet* for each team member.

4. Flip chart, markers, Sellotape or drawing pins.

Process

1. The facilitator forms teams of six (or they may be self-selected) and a leader is appointed for each team.

2. The facilitator gives a short description of the purpose of the activity and its underlying theory.

3. The facilitator gathers the leaders away from their teams, briefs them on their roles, and gives them a set of instructions and an envelope for each team member. Each envelope contains role descriptions for team members "B" to "F". The leader is given envelope "A" containing his or her role instructions.

4. Observers are appointed from team members who are not assigned roles "A" to "F". They are briefed by the facilitator regarding areas they should observe during the role play. Each observer will give a short debriefing following the exercise.

5. After two hours, the facilitator concludes the activity by having each group present their concert tour agendas and brochure element.

6. The facilitator wraps up the exercise by summarizing and giving a short briefing on team management skills.

Variations

Activity 38, Project Rescue, is another activity that focuses on the impact of personal agendas in team decisions.

TEAM LEADER INSTRUCTION SHEET

You have called a meeting of city tourism and entertainment representatives for six towns in a particular region: (a) Albertville, (b) Barreberg, (c) Cannonville, (d) Dale, (e) Edwardston and (f) Furntown. You are the representative of Albertville.

Each town will receive a percentage of the gate receipts based on the following process:

1. Order of Concert Stops

1st stop	=	30%
2nd stop	=	5%
3rd stop	=	15%
4th stop	=	15%
5th stop	=	5%
6th stop	=	30%

2. Appearances

3 nights	=	+10%
2 nights	=	+5%
1 night	=	+0%

DATA SHEET

You are an agent representing a town interested in developing a public concert series. You have been asked to agree on a six town tour for a new musical group. The following criteria apply:

1. Each agent has been asked by their town to ensure the maximum number of concerts for their town.

2. Each town will be allowed one town highlight in the brochure.

3. The concerts will be an eight day run.

4. Your group has to agree on the structure of the tour as follows:

    a. The order of the concert tour

    b. The number of concerts in each town

    c. The featured elements of each town in the brochure announcing the concert series

© Parker and Kropp, 1992. Published by Kogan Page.

ENVELOPE INSTRUCTIONS

Envelope A
You represent Albertville.

Albertville has the largest concert hall.

Albertville is halfway between the Regional Airport and the other towns.

Envelope B
You represent Barreberg.

Barreberg has a small but acoustically preferred concert hall.

Barreberg is a 3-hour drive from the Regional Airport.

The Albertville concert hall has a very poor sound

Envelope C
You represent Cannonville.

Cannonville uses an outdoor arena for concerts.

Furntown has no capacity to market the concert and must rely on the other five for help.

Envelope D
You represent Dale.

Dale is only 5 minutes from the Regional Airport.

Dale has limited hotel space.

Envelope E
You represent Edwardston.

Edwardston is located ten miles from Dale.

Edwardston has the smallest concert hall.

Envelope F
You represent Furntown.

Furntown has a medium sized concert hall.

Located in Furntown is a major resort and spa that attracts tourists from all over the world.

OBSERVATION GUIDE

Using this sheet as a guide observe the various roles, demonstrated behaviours and the impact those behaviours have on the success of each team member. Be prepared to provide feedback after the activity has been completed. Take notes.

To what extent were the following behaviours evident?

1. A clear team goal.

2. A clear communication structure.

3. Use of personal and hidden agendas.

4. Meeting management skills.

5. To what extent did the group achieve the goal?

   a. Order of the concert tour

   b. Number of concerts per town

   c. The featured brochure element

Activity 24
CREATING A TEAM MISSION

Purpose

1. To develop a shared view of a team's products or services.
2. To develop a shared view of a team's customers.
3. To create a team mission statement.
4. To train participants in preparing a mission statement.

Group Size

Works best with an intact team of four to eight people. In a team training workshop, the exercise can be done with up to fifteen people.

Time

One hour.

Physical Setting

Table and chairs arranged in U- shape.

Materials

1. Easel, flip chart, Sellotape or drawing pins
2. *Creating a Team Mission* for each person
3. *Criteria for Evaluating a Team Mission* for each person

Process

1. Explain the purpose of the activity.

95

2. Lecture on the content of a mission statement. A mission statement describes a team's main products or services and its customers. It answers the questions:

   • What do you do?

   • For whom do you do it?

   A mission statement can also reveal something about a team's values, its unique talents or type of technology.

3. Write the name of the team on a flip chart. Ask the group to brainstorm words and phrases that describe the team.

4. Record the responses in an organized fashion on the flip chart. Do not simply create a vertical list.

5. Ask each person to use the handout, *Creating a Team Mission,* and write one or two sentences that describe the team's products or services and their customers. They should use the "brainstormed" list for ideas, but they should not be restricted to those words and phrases.

6. Ask one person to present the team's statement. Write the statement on the flip chart.

7. Ask the team to clarify, discuss and edit the statement until they get close to a consensus on the words. Do not try to produce a final product.

8. Using the handout, *Evaluating a Team Mission*, ask the team to assess their statement against the criteria.

9. Conclude the session by saying that the draft statement will be typed and distributed to the team after the session.

10. At the next meeting they will discuss it again and reach a consensus on the final version of the statement.

Variations

1. Review the handout, *Evaluating a Team Mission*, prior to drafting the mission statement.

2. Ask a subcommittee to edit the draft after the session and bring it to the next team meeting.

3. A companion activity is Activity 30, Visioning a Vision.

CREATING A TEAM MISSION

The mission of_____ is to:

EVALUATING A TEAM MISSION

1. **Consistency:** Is it consistent with the corporate mission?

2. **Brevity:** Is it brief and to the point?

3. **Clarity:** Is it easy to understand?

4. **Specificity:** Does it reflect the unique character and flavour of your team?

5. **General:** Is it broad enough to include some growth and expansion of your particular products or services and your customer base?

6. **Pride:** Are you proud of it? Would you frame it and hang it in your work area? Show it to your boss? Your customers?

Activity 25
THE PRODUCT DEVELOPMENT TEAM

Purpose

1. To experience a team planning process.
2. To design and implement a team project.
3. To learn to give and receive team feedback.
4. To learn factors that help and hinder team decision making.

Group Size

A minimum of fifteen people. The activity is especially useful in a team training workshop but it can be used with an intact team.

Time

Two to three hours depending on group size and the number of teams in the workshop.

Physical Setting

Round or rectangular tables with chairs spread out around the room. It is important that the teams be unable to hear each other during the session. If necessary, break-out rooms can be used.

Materials

Team Reaction Form, Observer Guidelines, easel, flip chart and markers.

Process

1. Form teams of six or seven. Ask for two volunteers from each team to be observers. Explain the role of observers.
2. Brief the observers privately using the *Observer Guidelines*.

3. While you are meeting with the observers, you may ask the teams to develop a set of norms for team effectiveness which they will use during the exercise. See Activity 32, The Team of Your Life.

4. Ask each team to clear their table completely. Each team member is to place one small item from a pocket or handbag on the table (e.g., coin, pen, key).

5. Explain that the task is to develop a competitive game that can be played by two people using only the objects on their table. They must also plan to teach the game to two people who will actually play the game. Give teams a time limit of 30-45 minutes.

6. When the time period is over, ask team members to complete the *Team Reaction Form*. Observers join with the team members to give feedback and discuss the team's process during this period.

7. Have observers join a table they did not observe. They are taught the game that was created by that team. They play the game and give the team feedback on the game.

8. The observers rejoin their original team. The teams absorb the feedback and they use the information to revise the game. The observers continue to record their observations. Time limit: 15 minutes.

9. Observers then go to another team they did not observe (a different one from the team they moved to in step 7). They are now taught this game. They play the game and give feedback on the game to the team.

10. The observers return to their original team where they join with team members to discuss the process and summarize learnings on team planning, communication and decision making.

11. The facilitator asks each team for key learnings from this experience. The learnings are posted on the flip chart. The facilitator summarizes with a lecturette on team planning, listening, roles, and decision making.

Variations

1. Change step 4 to give all the teams the same items (e.g., paper clip, rubber band, watch, ring). The activity can be changed to a competitive exercise where the object is to create the best game.

2. A companion activity is Activity 1, Tricky Tales: A Cross-Team Building Approach.

TEAM REACTION FORM

1. How satisfied are you with the way your team planned the project?

| 1 | 2 | 3 | 4 | 5 |

Very
Dissatisfied

Very
Satisfied

Comments:

2. How satisfied are you with the way the team utilized its resources (material and human)?

| 1 | 2 | 3 | 4 | 5 |

Very
Dissatisfied

Very
Satisfied

Comments:

3. Comment to the extent to which team members:

    a.   Were focused on the task and shared their experience.

    b.   Saw the "big picture" and addressed strategic issues.

    c.   Were concerned about team dynamics and positive goals and method.

    d.   Raised important questions about team goals and methods.

101

4. What things helped the team?

5. What things hindered team effectiveness?

6. How can we increase team effectiveness?

OBSERVER GUIDELINES

1. Sit where you can see and hear most of the team.

2. Take notes—include quotes where possible. Note the things that *help* and *hinder* the team and the *impact* of what was said or done.

   TASK ORIENTED BEHAVIOUR (keeping focused on the job to be done)

   STRATEGIC BEHAVIOUR (seeing the big picture)

   PROCESS BEHAVIOUR (how the team is working together)

CHALLENGING BEHAVIOUR (effectively disagreeing with others)

NON-VERBAL BEHAVIOUR (communicating without words)

DYSFUNCTIONAL BEHAVIOUR (e.g., side conversation, monopolizing)

Activity 26
TRANSITION TEAM
BUILDING

Purpose

1. To smooth the transition of leadership in a team.
2. To quickly integrate a new team leader.

Group Size

Works best with a team of four to eight people but can be used with up to twelve people. This activity is only used with intact teams.

Time

Two hours in addition to time for data collection interviews.

Physical Setting

Round or rectangular tables and chairs. The room should have sufficient wall space to post flip chart paper.

Materials

Easel, flip chart, markers, and Sellotape or drawing pins.

Process

1. Prior to the session, interview each team member using these questions:
   - What questions and concerns do you have about the new team leader?
   - What concerns do you have about the current leader leaving?

   Tell team members they will be expected to present a brief description of their particular job and current projects at the transition team meeting.
2. Prior to the session meet with the current leader and brief him/her on the purpose and format. Ask him/her to prepare a brief summary of the current priorities and future plans of the team.

105

3. Prior to the session meet with the new leader and brief him/her on the session. Indicate that he/she will be asked to present a summary of his/her background and a description of leadership style.

4. The agenda for the meeting is:

   a. Presentations by team members. The new leader may ask questions for clarification.

   b. Presentation by current team leader.

   c. Presentation by new team leader.

   d. Data feedback on concerns/questions from interviews (posted on flip charts).

   e. Responses by the new and current team leader.

5. The session concludes with a summary by the facilitator and review of next steps and action items generated by the discussion.

Variations

1. If the current leader has left and is not available, the session may be held just with the new leader using the same process.

2. If interviews cannot be held prior to the session, ask the new team leader to leave the room for 15 minutes, or arrive 15 minutes after the meeting begins. Then ask the team to develop a list of questions and concerns. Record on a flip chart and go through them when the leader returns.

3. See Activity 3, Getting to Know The Boss, for a similar activity.

Activity 27
FORMING NEW TEAMS

Purpose

1. To quickly form new teams with strangers or people who do not usually work together.
2. To learn factors that help and hinder team problem-solving and decision-making.
3. To get acquainted with other participants at a conference or company meeting.

Group Size

Any size group.

Time

Forty-five minutes to one hour.

Physical Setting

Large room with movable chairs.

Materials

Copies of the following for each person:

1. *Getting to Know You.*
2. *The Things You Know You Know.*
3. *Team Process Review.*

Process

1. As each person arrives, give him/her a card with a name on it that is part of a pair of names. See *Ideas for Pairs* handout. Make sure that people who know each other are not paired.

107

2. Explain the purpose of the activity. Ask participants to take out their card and find their partner.

3. Once they find their partner they are to use the *Getting to Know You* handout to facilitate their discussion.

4. After 10 to 15 minutes, ask the pairs to find another pair and introduce their partners to each other.

5. After about 15 minutes distribute the *Things You Know You Know* handout. Explain that the task is to use their team resources to answer the questions.

6. When they have answered the questions, give each person a copy of *Team Process Review* and ask them to complete it.

7. The teams should use the form as a basis for discussion of factors that help and hinder team effectiveness.

8. Conclude the session by asking the group for key learning from the experience. Post the points on a flip chart or transparency. The facilitator should add points not sufficiently covered.

9. Give people the answers to *The Things You Know You Know* questions.

Variations

1. Change the *Things You Know You Know* to questions about the company, industry or a related topic.

2. Change the pairs to countries and their capitals.

3. In step 4 ask the pairs to join with two other pairs to form a team of six people.

4. Make it a competitive exercise with the first team to get all the correct answers declared the winner. Give the winning team a prize.

5. Change it to a get-acquainted activity by stopping at step 3.

6. Eliminate the *Team Process Review.*

7. Other get acquainted activities are Activity 2, Yea Team!; Activity 21, Darts; and Activity 44, That's Me.

IDEAS FOR PAIRS

1. Romeo and Juliet
2. Rolls and Royce
3. Pinky and Perky
4. Butch Cassidy and the Sundance Kid
5. Salt and Pepper
6. June Whitfield and Terry Scott
7. Morecambe and Wise
8. Bacon and Eggs
9. Rommel and Montgomery
10. Tom and Jerry
11. King and Queen
12. Rhythm and Blues
13. Laurel and Hardy
14. Rosencrantz and Guildenstern
15. Oxford and Cambridge
16. Elizabeth Barrett and Robert Browning
17. Fish and Chips
18. Popeye and Olive Oil
19. Merchant and Ivory
20. Bangers and Mash
21. Sonny and Cher
22. Saatchi and Saatchi
23. Bonnie and Clyde
24. Benson and Hedges
25. Simon and Garfunkel
26. Mork and Mindy
27. Antony and Cleopatra
28. Marks and Spencer
29. Gin and Tonic
30. Beer and Skittles

GETTING TO KNOW YOU

The purpose of this meeting is to get to know the other person. Use these questions as a guide only. Feel free to ask and answer other questions that interest you.

1. Where were you born? Where were you brought up?

2. What is your job? What do you like best about it? What would you change about it?

3. Are you married? Do you have a family?

4. What are your hobbies and outside interests?

5. Where did you go on your last holiday? Where are you going this year?

6. If you could change occupations, what would you do?

7. Other questions (e.g., How do you feel about this meeting? How do you feel about this exercise?).

THE THINGS YOU KNOW YOU KNOW

1. What are the 12 signs of the zodiac?

2. Who was the first man to orbit the earth?

3. Name the seven deadly sins.

4. What are the names of the planets, beginning with the one closest to the sun?

5. What is the longest river in the world and what continent is it in?

ANSWER SHEET

1. The twelve signs of the zodiac are:

Aries	Libra
Taurus	Scorpio
Gemini	Sagittarius
Cancer	Capricorn
Leo	Aquarius
Virgo	Pisces

2. Yuri Gagarin, in 1961

3. The seven Deadly Sins are:

Pride	Gluttony
Covetousness	Envy
Lust	Sloth
Anger	

4. The names of the planets are:

Mercury

Venus

Earth

Mars

Jupiter

Saturn

Uranus

Neptune

Pluto

5. The longest river is the Nile in Africa.

TEAM PROCESS REVIEW

1. What did your team do that helped complete the task?

2. What things hindered the completion of the task?

3. What would you do differently next time?

4. What did you learn about team effectiveness?

Activity 28

LINKING TEAM PROBLEM SOLVING WITH CORPORATE STRATEGY

Purpose

1. To learn a structured team problem-solving process.

2. To align team problem-solving with current business strategy.

3. To solve an actual business problem.

Group Size

An intact team of six to eight people or several teams of six to eight who are attending a team training workshop.

Time

One day in addition to time for pre-work and post-meeting follow up.

Physical Setting

For team building a small room with a round or rectangular table and chairs. For team training a large room with several sets of tables and chairs spread out around the room.

Materials

1. Easel, flip chart, markers, Sellotape or drawing pins, overhead projector, screen, blank transparencies and projector pens.

2. A copy of your corporate strategy statement and the *Project Outline* for each person.

115

Process

1. Prior to the session give each person a copy of your corporate strategy statement and ask them to think of problems that are barriers to the achievement of one or more of the strategies.

2. Explain the purpose of the session. Review the strategies or ask a top manager to attend and conduct the review. Ask the participants if they have questions or need a clarification of any of the strategies.

3. Review the *Project Outline*. Explain that at _o'clock (two hours prior to the end of the session) they will have to present their project plan to a panel of top managers. The managers will listen, ask questions and offer suggestions. The problem selected by the team must be related to one of the strategies and the problem solution must move the organization toward the achievement of the strategy. The time table for completion of the project must not exceed 90 days.

4. The team(s) spend the remainder of the time preparing their *Project Outline* and presentation.

5. A panel of top managers has been contacted and briefed in advance of the session. They arrive at the appointed time and listen to the presentations. They provide feedback as appropriate.

6. The panel departs and the facilitator leads a debriefing session with the team(s).

7. During the next 90 days the team(s) work on completing their projects.

8. At the appropriate time the teams report to a group of top managers or just to the panel that participated in the workshop.

Variations

1. A top manager from the panel may be appointed to serve as an advisor to the team.

2. The top management team may create a list of problems from which the teams can choose.

3. In a team training workshop you may want to begin with an ice-breaker activity such as Activity 32, The Team of Your Life or Activity 27, Forming New Teams.

PROJECT OUTLINE

1. Problem Statement

2. Benefits

3. Related Corporate Strategy

4. Action Steps

5. Resources Needed

6. Obstacles

7. Timetable

8. Final Product

Activity 29
TEAM BUILDING INTERVIEW GUIDE

Purpose

1. To collect data on the strengths and weaknesses of the team.
2. To collect data to plan a team building intervention.
3. To explain the team building process to the participants.

Group Size

The suggested format is individual interviews. Therefore, a maximum of twelve or, at most, fifteen people is recommended. Beyond this size, a written survey is the preferred data gathering tool.

Time

A minimum of thirty minutes and a maximum of one hour for each interview.

Physical Setting

A private office or small meeting room.

Materials

A sufficient number of blank copies of the *Team Building Interview Guide*.

Process

1. Begin the meeting by introducing yourself, your role as a team building consultant, the purpose of the interview, the format of the interview, what will happen to the data, who will see the data, how it will be used in the team building process and the confidential nature of the interview.
2. Give the person a copy of the form and explain that you will ask the questions on the form and write the answers on your copy.

119

3. If you do not know the person, you may wish to begin by asking him or her for a job description. Then move on to the questions on the *Team Building Interview Guide*. Probe and follow-up on answers as appropriate.

4. At the end of the interview, go back over the form and review your notes with the person. Ask if you have accurately captured his/her ideas and opinions. Review what will happen to the data and what are the next steps in the team building process.

5. Thank the person.

6. Review your notes before the next interview and add any final thoughts.

Variations

1. If conditions do not allow for individual interviews, use the *Team Building Interview Guide* to conduct a series of small group interviews. Record the answers on a flip chart.

2. Add or delete questions to tailor the guide to your specific team. For example, with a new team you may want to ask about concerns people have about being on a new or start-up team. With a cross-functional team you may want to ask about relationships with people from other parts of the company.

3. An alternative approach is to use a survey instrument. See Activity 15, Characteristics of an Effective Work Team: An Assessment Activity.

TEAM BUILDING INTERVIEW GUIDE

1. Briefly describe your team(s) in terms of membership, structure, purpose.

2. What are the key challenges facing your team?

3. What do you see as the strengths of your team?

4. What areas need improvement?

5. What changes would make the team more effective? (Probe for things the team can do and things the organization can do to support the team.)

6. Are the roles clear? Is everyone clear about what is expected from them?

7. How would you describe team meetings? Are improvements needed?

8. How does your team handle internal conflict?

9. How does your team interact with other teams, clients and key stakeholders in the organization?

10. What would make this team building session successful for you? What would you like to see happen as a result of the session? What would you personally like to walk away with?

11. Wha else should I know that would help to make this event successful?

Activity 30
VISIONING A VISION

Purpose

1. To create a future focus for the team.
2. To develop the first step in a strategic planning process.
3. To create a vision statement for the team.

Group Size

Works effectively with an intact team of four to eight people. For a team training workshop, a maximum of fifteen is recommended.

Time

Two hours.

Physical Setting

A small classroom with sufficient blank walls to post up to 15 sheets of flip chart paper.

Materials

Easel, flip chart, markers (one for each person) and Sellotape or drawing pins.

Process

1. Facilitator explains the purpose of a vision as a "statement of a team's *preferred* future as opposed to its *predicted* future." A vision is what you want and hope the team will become. It reflects your hopes, dreams and aspirations. Visioning is a free-form, brainstorming process in which you create the future you want.

2. Begin by asking people to relax, even close their eyes, and consider this scenario (you may wish to play some quiet music):

   • It is five years from now (the year ____). You are in a helicopter hovering over ____. What would you like to see? What would please you? What are we doing? How are we working? With whom are we working? What does the work environment look like?

   • Once you get some images in mind, write them down. Feel free to draw a picture, a cartoon, a chart or a list.

   • Take a sheet of flip chart paper, a marker and some pins or tape. Transcribe your vision to the paper and post it on the wall. Don't forget to sign it.

3. When everyone has posted his/her vision, ask the entire team to walk around and view the "exhibit." Ask them to look for common themes, surprises, good ideas, and other things that should be included in a shared team vision.

4. When the group comes together, ask for ideas to be included in a shared team vision. Post the ideas on a flip chart. Probe for commitment to the resulting vision statement.

5. Close the session by restating the purpose of a shared vision. Suggest that the team have the vision statement printed and distributed to everyone following the session. Suggest further that the team reconvene within a week to review and commit to the statement.

Variations

1. At the end of the session, each person can come up and sign the vision statement on the flip chart as a gesture symbolizing enrolment in the vision.

2. At the end of the session, or at the follow-up session, each person can indicate what he/she plans to do to make the vision a reality.

3. A possible next activity for this team would be Activity 24, Creating a Team Mission.

Activity 31
A "PRESCRIPTION" FOR TEAM EFFECTIVENESS

Purpose

1. To provide feedback to each team member.
2. To develop an action plan for self-development for each person.
3. To close a team building session.

Group Size

Works best with an intact team of four to eight people. Can be used in a team training workshop if the class has been working in small teams during the programme.

Time

One hour.

Physical Setting

Tables and chairs since the activity requires writing.

Materials

1. Pencil or pen for each person.
2. 3" x 5" cards so that each person has enough cards to prepare a "prescription" for everyone in the group.
3. Envelopes so that each person has one with his/her name on it.

Process

1. Explain the purpose and format of the activity. Distribute the cards and pencils.

125

2. Each person is asked to prepare a "prescription" for every other person on the team, suggesting what the person should:

    a.   continue doing because it is helpful to the team.

    b.   stop doing because it is hurting the team.

    c.   start doing because it would help the team.

3. Take the envelopes—each with a person's name on it— and collect all corresponding prescriptions prepared by the team. Give each person his/her envelope with all the cards.

4. Each person should read the cards and prepare his/her own prescription.

5. You may ask each person to share his/her personal prescription.

Variations

1. If the team is ready to be completely open, the prescriptions can be verbal instead of written. In this variation, start with one person to give him or her feedback using the same three areas (continue, stop, start).

2. If the team is ready to completely open up, the prescription can be written on flip chart paper. The facilitator posts one piece of paper for each person on the wall. Team members write their prescription for each person on their flip chart.

3. Limit the prescriptions to only positive items. In others, the items written on the cards must be strengths—things the person does that help the team and should be continued.

Activity 32
THE TEAM OF YOUR LIFE

Purpose

1. To share positive experiences as a member of a team.
2. To develop a shared understanding of team success factors.
3. To develop a list of team norms.

Group Size

Works effectively with a team of four to eight people. It can also be used in a team training workshop with a large number of people. In that case the class should be divided into teams of six to nine people.

Time

Thirty minutes to one hour depending on the number of team members.

Physical Setting

Team building with one team: small room with a round or rectangular table and chairs or chairs only, arranged in a circle. For a team training workshop: round or rectangular tables and chairs spread out around the room.

Materials

1. Easel, flip chart and markers.
2. For a team training workshop, each team will need an easel or just flip chart paper, markers, and Sellotape or drawing pins.

Process

1. Facilitator explains the purpose of the activity and that the participants' experiences on teams will be used to help understand the dimensions of an effective team.

2. Facilitator explains that each person will be asked to:

   a. describe his/her best experience as a team member—either formal, informal, on-the-job, or off-the-job.

   b. explain what made the experience "special"—what happened, what worked, what specific things did the team do?

3. Facilitator explains that after the experiences have been shared the team will create a list of team norms. The team should draw on their positive experiences to develop the list. In other words, what positive things from their past experiences do they want to bring to this team? The facilitator explains that norms are "standards of behaviour a team expects of its members." They are guidelines for acceptable behaviour.

4. Team members share their experiences and the team develops its list of norms. In a team training class, each team may share its list of norms with the total group.

5. The facilitator closes the session by saying that the norms now become the guidelines by which the team will live for as long as they like. They may be revised periodically.

Variations

1. Team members may share their "worst" experience on a team.

2. The team norms may be developed by creating two columns:

WANTS	DON'T WANTS

128

Activity 33
I THINK I MAKE A CONTRIBUTION

Purpose

1. To expand team members' awareness of their contribution to the team.
2. To experience feedback on personal contribution.

Group Size

Eight to twelve team members.

Time

Up to two hours.

Materials

1. Paper, pencils, Sellotape or drawing pins for each member.
2. Ranking cards made from A4 sheets. Each card should have a separate number on it so that the numbers 1 to 7 each has its own card.
3. Flip chart paper and markers.

Physical Setting

A room large enough to post ranking cards on the walls. Arrange the ranking cards from 1 to 7 horizontally along a wall.

Process

1. The facilitator asks each team member to reflect for a few minutes about his/her own contribution to the team's ability to achieve its purpose. Each member should arrive at a rank level for the contribution. A ranking of 1 indicates little contribution to the team, and a ranking of 7 indicates high contribution to the team's ability to achieve its purpose.
2. The facilitator asks the team leader to reflect on each team member's contributions to the team's ability to achieve its purpose.

129

3. The facilitator then asks the team members to go to the wall where the ranking cards are posted and stand below the card that they feel reflects their contribution to the team.

4. Each member will be asked in turn to explain the reasons why they ranked themselves in their particular position and how they arrived at their decision.

5. The team leader will then record the individual rankings on the *Summary Sheet*.

6. The team leader will then arrange the team members in the positions that he/she decided upon during the reflection period. The leader will discuss the reasons why rankings were different or the same as the individual member's ranking.

7. The leader and the individual members develop action plans that will increase each person's contribution to the team's ability to achieve its purpose.

Variations

1. The team leader step (6) is omitted.

2. The number of rounds may be varied.

3. Other traits (e.g., communication or listening) may be substituted.

4. Another personal feedback activity is Activity 31, A "Prescription" for Team Effectiveness.

SUMMARY SHEET

Rank each team member according to your assessment of his/her contribution to the overall success of your team. A ranking of 1 indicates limited contribution, a ranking of 7 indicates high contribution.

TEAM LEADER RANKINGS

1	2	3	4	5	6	7

INDIVIDUAL MEMBER RANKINGS

1	2	3	4	5	6	7

Activity 34
TEAM ON TEAM

Purpose

1. To develop skills in team process observation.

2. To develop skills in giving and receiving feedback in interdependent team situations.

3. To become more aware of key communication skills required of all successful teams.

Group Size

Two (or even-numbered) interdependent teams of five to eight people.

Time

At least sixty minutes but no longer than ninety minutes.

Physical Setting

The two groups sit in circles facing inward.

Materials

1. Paper and pens for observers.

2. *Process Observation Guide.*

Process

1. The facilitator asks the teams to be seated in circles and explains the purpose of the exercise describing the general sequences of events.

2. One team is seated as the inner circle and the other team as the outer circle.

3. The facilitator instructs members of the outer circle to observe one (or more) inner circle participants' effectiveness in the group discussion using the *Process Observation Guide*. The facilitator explains each of the eight items included in the *Guide*. Observers are encouraged to take notes on examples of each of the items.

4. The facilitator assigns a discussion topic relevant to the groups.

5. After about 15 minutes, the facilitator asks the participants and the observers to pair off and meet privately to give feedback and discuss the process.

6. The process is reversed so that the inner circle team becomes the outer circle. The facilitator assigns a new topic.

7. After about 15 minutes, the inner circle participants and the observers meet to give feedback and discuss the process.

8. The group is reassembled and the entire process is discussed.

Variations

1. Observer may be given specific skills to look for based on pre-session needs assessment.

2. An alternative activity is Activity 45, The Effective Team Member: A Consensus Activity.

PROCESS OBSERVATION GUIDE

TEAM MEMBER'S NAME   DATE

COMMUNICATION AWARENESS	Low				High
1. Listening	1	2	3	4	5
2. Responding	1	2	3	4	5
3. Oral presentation	1	2	3	4	5
4. Non-verbal presentation	1	2	3	4	5

TEAM ROLE	Low				High
1. Leadership	1	2	3	4	5
2. Followership	1	2	3	4	5
3. Response to leadership	1	2	3	4	5
4. Response to followership	1	2	3	4	5

Activity 35
TEAM DEVELOPMENT:
A GRID PERSPECTIVE

Purpose

1. To diagnose and evaluate the stage of development of an intact work team.
2. To compare team development with performance independence.
3. To compare team members' perceptions of team development at a given time.

Group Size

A team of seven to twelve is best, but larger teams can be organized into subgroups and final grids compared.

Time

One hour.

Physical Setting

Tables and chairs arranged in a conference or U-shape.

Materials

1. Pencils/marking pens.
2. Copies of *Team Development Grid*.
3. Easel and flip chart.

Process

1. The team leader gives a briefing on team development stressing the notion of interdependence and the need to become self-directed. The team leader also discusses the process of self-renewal.

137

2. The team leader asks each member to review the *Team Development Grid* explaining the Self Direction Axis and the Self Renewal Axis. The team leader explains that in order to complete the team development grid, each team member plots his/her perception of the team's self directedness, and self renewal, and locates the intersection of the scores they have assigned. For example, if they believe that the team is 75% self directed, and 50% self-renewing, they would place a mark in the upper left-hand quadrant of the grid.

3. The team members post up their work and the group at large discusses the team members' perceptions.

4. The team develops an action plan to achieve a high level of self direction and self renewal.

TEAM DEVELOPMENT GRID

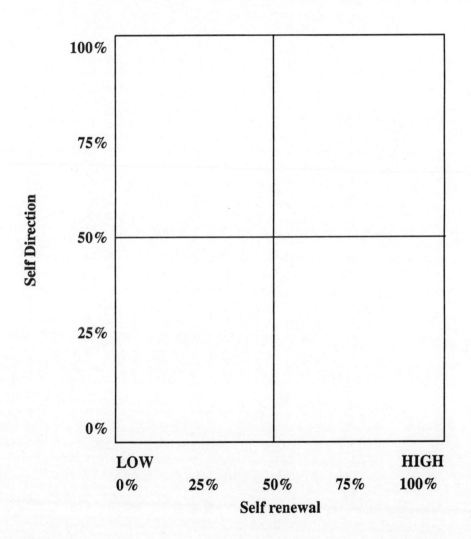

139

Activity 36
SELECTING A PROBLEM SOLUTION

Purpose

1. To teach a team or team leaders the factors that should be considered in selecting the best solution to a problem.

2. To teach a team or team leaders a process for deciding among various alternative solutions to a problem.

Group Size

Works best with an intact team of four to twelve people or in a team training workshop of up to twenty people.

Time

One to two hours.

Physical Setting

With an intact team, a round or rectangular table and chairs.

In a training workshop, groups of tables and chairs spread around the room.

Materials

1. A copy of the *Ratings Scales* for each person.

2. A copy of the *Problem Solution Work Sheet* for each person.

3. Easel, flip chart, and markers.

Process

1. This activity takes place after a team has generated several solutions to a problem.

141

2. Distribute a copy of the *Problem Solution Work Sheet* to each person. Tell the team to write a brief description of each solution in the left column of the work sheet. If necessary, explain what is meant by each of the factors across the top of the work sheet. Special attention should be given to types of typical costs (labour, materials) and benefits (costs reduction, quality improvement).

3. Post the totals for each solution on a flip chart. Lead a discussion on each of the solutions by focusing on the relative importance of the factors.

4. Move the discussion toward a consensus on one solution. Suggest that the next step will be the development of an action plan for implementing the solution.

Variations

1. Each person completes the work sheet prior to the session.

2. In a team training session, case materials using a simulated problem and possible solutions can be created for this exercise.

RATING SCALES

BENEFITS	COST	EASE OF IMPLEMENTATION	TIME	SECONDARY IMPACTS
1. The expected benefits will be minimal.	1. The cost will be very high.	1. It will be very difficult to implement.	1. It will be more than 6 months before benefits are seen.	1. It also results in some significant negative impacts.
2. The expected benefits will be good.	2. The cost will be high.	2. It will be difficult to implement.	2. It will be 3 to 6 months before benefits are seen.	2. It also results in some negative impacts.
3. The expected benefits will be very good.	3. The cost will be low.	3. There will be a few obstacles to putting it into practice.	3. It will be 1 to 3 months before benefits are seen.	3. It also results in additional positive impacts.
4. The expected benefits will be outstanding.	4. There will be no added cost.	4. It can be easily put into practice.	4. Benefits will be seen in less than 30 days.	4. It also results in some additional significant positive impacts.

DIRECTIONS

1. Prior to rating the solutions, discuss the categories as they relate to the problems to make sure that everyone is clear about their meaning.

2. List the solutions in the column to the left. It is assumed that they all adequately solve the problem.

3. Using the above scales, rate each problem in the five categories and compute the total.

4. Develop a team score for each solution by sharing your individual ratings for each category and then computing a total. (It may be useful to post the ratings on a flip chart and then discuss the reasons for each.)

5. Circle the highest rated solution and proceed to the preparation of an action plan.

PROBLEM SOLUTION WORK SHEET

	SOLUTION DESCRIPTION	BENEFITS	COSTS	EASE OF IMPLEMENTATION	TIME	SECONDARY IMPACTS	TOTAL
1							
2							
3							
4							
5							

144

Activity 37
SELECTING A TEAM
PROBLEM

Purpose

1. To teach a team or team leaders the factors that should be considered in selecting a problem to solve.
2. To teach a team or team leaders a process for deciding which problem the team should try to solve.

Group Size

Works best with a team of four to twelve people or in a team training workshop of up to twenty people.

Time

One to two hours.

Physical Setting

With a team, a round or rectangular table and chairs.

In a training workshop, groups of tables and chairs spread out around the room.

Materials

1. A copy of the *Problem Selection Work Sheet* and *Rating Scales* for each person.
2. An easel, flip chart and markers.

Process

1. This activity takes place after the team has brainstormed or in some other way generated a list of problems.

145

2. Distribute a copy of the *Problem Selection Work Sheet* to each person. Tell the team to write a brief description of the problem in the left column of the work sheet. Review the directions on the work sheet. If necessary, review what is meant by each of the factors across the top of the work sheet.

3. Post the totals for each problem on a flip chart. Lead a discussion on each of the problems by focusing on the relative importance of each of the factors.

4. Move the discussion to a consensus on one of the problems. Suggest that the next step is the creation of a clear problem statement. See Activity 11, The Car Case, for an exercise on writing problem statements.

PROBLEM SELECTION WORK SHEET

Problem	Under/Not Under Team's Control	Important/ Unimportant	Easy/Hard	Time	Projected ROI	Total
1.						
2.						
3.						
4.						
5.						
6.						
7.						
8.						
9.						
10.						
11.						
12.						
13.						
14.						
15.						

RATING SCALES

UNDER/NOT UNDER CONTROL	IMPORTANT/ UNIMPORTANT	EASY/HARD	TIME	PROJECTED RETURN ON INVESTMENT (ROI)
1. Our team has no control over this problem.	1. If relevant, it's not obvious.	1. Possible, but very hard to solve.	1. Over 6 months.	1. No expected payoff for effort required.
2. Our team has some control over this problem.	2. Might have some importance for our area.	2. Will take considerable time and effort.	2. 3–6 months.	2. Some expected payoff for effort required.
3. Our team has considerable control over this problem.	3. Has considerable importance for our area.	3. Will take some time and effort.	3. 1–2 months.	3. Considerable expected payoff for effort required.
4. Our team has almost complete control over this problem.	4. Extremely important.	4. Really easy to solve.	4. Less than 1 month.	4. Great expected benefit for effort required.

DIRECTIONS

1. In each of the five categories listed above, determine an appropriate score for each problem being considered.
2. Develop a total team score for each problem by adding together all of your five individual scores. (Place this total score in the column at the far right of the page.)
3. Develop a total team score for each problem to determine a team ranking for all problems.
4. Using this ranking process as a guide, discuss reasons for specific ratings, then finalize a potential to work on.

148

Activity 38
PROJECT RESCUE

Purpose

1. To explore the dynamics of problem solving and decision making.
2. To become aware of team planning and role clarification.
3. To become aware of cross-functional interdependencies.

Group Size

Designed for a team training workshop with the participants divided into teams of five people each. The total number of participants is limited only by the space available and the ability of the facilitator to handle large groups.

Time

One to two hours.

Physical Setting

A room large enough for the groups to work comfortably; round or rectangular tables with chairs.

Materials

1. Easel, flip charts, markers and Sellotape or drawing pins for each team.
2. Copies of *Background Sheet* for each team member.
3. Individual *Role Sheets*.

Process

1. The facilitator gives a short talk on the need for collaboration and open communication to ensure overall team effectiveness. Further, the facilitator briefs the group on the concept of team formation and the need to clarify roles and establish team norms.

149

2. The facilitator forms groups of five and explains the activity, indicating that team members should not share their role sheet information sets with one another until after the activity has been completed.

3. The facilitator begins the activity and then monitors each team's progress and process.

4. After sixty minutes the facilitator concludes the activity asking each group to describe their work and leads a discussion on role conflict, team problem-solving, and team decision-making.

Variations

1. Change the *Role Sheets* to include typical roles on your teams.

2. Revise the case description to reflect current issues in your organization.

3. Related activities are Activity 25, The Product Development Team and Activity 23, The Victory Tour.

BACKGROUND SHEET

You are an employee of DGI, Inc., a company that has been in business for nearly 50 years and manufactures sandpaper (as well as other products). DGI is located in the city of Lyttleville. Because of the nature of the product, serious questions have been raised about the company's ability to compete in a global economy. The managing director has asked a group of people to come together to develop a strategy to ensure the company's long-term success.

You have been asked to join this group. The group's first meeting is today.

151

ROLE SHEETS

Role Sheet 1

The Sales Rep

You have been appointed to serve on the task force representing the sales and marketing function. Your goal is to take control of the team using a power mode to influence what you believe the current market demands to be.

The Product Development Rep

You have been appointed to serve on the task team representing R & D. Your goal is to keep the company in the same product line because you believe it to be correct.

The Manufacturing Rep

You have been appointed to serve on the task team representing the manufacturing unit. Your goal is to maintain the status quo from a product standpoint but you believe that expansion of the manufacturing operation to the Far East is the best way to go global.

The Finance Rep

You have been appointed the finance rep. Your goal is to reduce inventory levels and you will fight any effort to redirect the company if you believe the move to be prohibitive.

The HR Rep

You have been asked to join the team to ensure that human aspects of the future are considered.

Activity 39
ROADBLOCKS: A CONSTRAINT ACTIVITY

Purpose

To become aware of the various roadblocks that can constrain team effectiveness.

Group Size

Fifteen to thirty people in a team workshop.

Time

One hour.

Physical Setting

A room large enough for the entire group as well as break-out rooms for subgroups.

Materials

1. Easel, flip chart and markers for each group.
2. *Leader Instruction Sheet* for each group.
3. Role descriptions for each team leader. Each role description can be printed on a 3" x 5" index card. See the *Role Description Sheet*.
4. Copies of the *Situation Work Sheet* for each participant.
5. Copies of the *Observers' Work Sheet* for three observers.

Process

1. The facilitator gives a brief talk on how road blocks can constrain a team from reaching its goals and objectives.
2. The facilitator explains the purpose of the activity and the agenda.

153

3. The facilitator selects three people to serve as team leaders. The team leaders are given a *Leader Instruction Sheet*, one *Role Description Sheet* and a *Situation Work Sheet*. The team leaders then go off for five minutes to review the handouts.

4. The facilitator selects three participants to be observers and reviews the *Observers' Work Sheet* with them.

5. The facilitator assigns the remaining participants to a team and gives each person a copy of the *Situation Work Sheet*.

6. The team leaders return and begin the activity.

7. After 20 minutes the meetings are ended. The observers provide feedback and discuss the impact of the leader's behaviour on the team.

8. The teams reassemble to discuss the roadblocks and the process used to deal with them.

Variations

1. A work team issue can be used as the basis for the activity.

2. Other activities where hidden agendas have an impact on team decisions include Activity 38, Project Rescue and Activity 23, The Victory Tour.

ROLE DESCRIPTION SHEET

Roadblocks Leader's Role 1

- You expect well developed solutions that are practical, logical and a credit to you and your ability to manage the team.
- You want to achieve consensus.

Roadblocks Leader's Role 2

- You don't really want a solution and will stall as long as possible.
- You can use the "We have already tried that one before," "It will cost too much" and other similar "idea killers" to block the team.
- Your intent is to reject suggestions.

Roadblocks Leader's Role 3

- You have a preconceived solution.
- You consider any suggestion a weakening of your idea. Therefore, minimize other ideas unless they could enhance your idea.
- You don't want the group to know you have a pre-selected solution.

LEADER INSTRUCTION SHEET

1. Read your role description. Learn your role. Feel free to add ideas and opinions as long as they are consistent with your basic role.

2. Don't reveal your role data to anyone. Stay in your role for the duration of the exercise.

3. Don't overact.

SITUATION WORK SHEET

There is movement in the company to open a new production facility in a city located 50 miles from the company headquarters. A number of issues have been raised by various groups—employees, townspeople, stockholders and public officials. Some of these issues are:

1. Who will staff the new plant?
2. What will happen to the production plant at the company headquarters?
3. How will the traffic be managed? There seems to be limited access to this new location.

Your team has been asked to develop and present ideas on how to identify and solve the problems to this new production facility.

OBSERVERS' WORK SHEET

1. How would you describe the leader's behaviour during the meeting?

2. What impact did the leader's behaviour have on the group?

3. How far did the team get in reaching its objective?

4. How could the team have been more successful?

Activity 40
THE QUALITY CASE: AN ETHICAL DILEMMA

Purpose
1. To teach an ethical decision-making model for teams.
2. To explore the factors involved in resolving an ethical dilemma.

Group Size
Works best with team building or team training groups of four to twelve.

Time
One and a half hours.

Physical Setting
Round or rectangular tables and chairs.

Materials
A copy of *The Quality Case* and *Factors in Team Ethics* for each person.

Process
1. Explain the purpose of the exercise. Brainstorm ethical issues for teams. Discuss the list.
2. Distribute *Factors in Team Ethics*. Review and explain each factor. Ask the participants for examples that illustrate each factor (e.g., "What laws and regulations affect our work?")
3. Distribute *The Quality Case*. Ask the team to analyse the case and decide what they would do. The team should use the factors as a guide in analysing the case.

159

4. The team presents its analysis and decision. Group discussion follows with the facilitator probing for reasons and other alternatives.

5. The session concludes with a discussion of the implications for team effectiveness which emerge from the activity.

Variations

1. Revise the case or create a new case which more closely relates to the work of the team.

2. The team analyses the case prior to the presentation of the *Factors* hand-out. Review the *Factors* after the team presents its solution. Discuss the case again in light of the factors.

THE QUALITY CASE

Your team is responsible for the development of a new system. The team has contracted with a user group for a specific set of requirements and delivery date.

At a team meeting just prior to the delivery date, several team members argue that the system is not up to their usual standards of quality. They do not want to deploy the system because it still has some problems. Other team members want to deliver the system on the due date in order to meet the commitment. They say that while it still has some problems, it does meet the user's requirements. The others agree that the system does, in fact, meet the requirements but they say the team should not allow work of questionable quality to "go public."

- What is the dilemma?

- Who are the stakeholders?

- What factors should the team consider in making its decision?

- What should the team do?

FACTORS IN TEAM ETHICS

1. Laws, regulations, possible legal liability.

2. Professional standards and ethical codes of conduct.

3. Corporate policies and procedures.

4. Corporate culture and organizational norms.

5. Personal and team values.

Activity 41
TOUGH JOBS

Purpose

1. To assess the degree to which members of a team can agree on a data set.
2. To teach the process of consensus decision-making.

Group Size

Effective either as a team building activity with an intact team of five to seven people or in a team training workshop with several teams of five to seven people.

Time

Two hours.

Physical Setting

A room large enough for break-out sessions of five to seven people each.

Materials

1. Copy of the *Ranking Sheet*.
2. Flip chart and marker.
3. *Consensus Decision-Making Process Review*.
4. *Answer Sheet*.

Process

1. The facilitator forms groups and explains the activity.
2. Each team member is given a *Ranking Sheet* and is asked to privately rank the jobs according to the degree of danger in the job. The most dangerous job is ranked "1" and so on to a rank of "10" for the least dangerous job.

© Parker and Kropp, 1992. Published by Kogan Page.

3. Once the individual rankings have been completed the team is asked to develop a team ranking of the jobs. Allow 30 minutes.

4. Distribute *Consensus Decision-Making Process Review*. Ask each person to complete the form, but not discuss it.

5. Present the *Answer Sheet*. The answers should be listed in column 3 on the ranking sheet. Ask the teams to complete column 4 and 5 including the totals.

6. Post a flip chart with the scores from each team as follows:

	Team A	Team B	Team C
Average Individual Score			
Team Score (column 5)			
Difference			

7. The facilitator should lead a discussion on the reasons for the difference between the average individual score and the team score.

8. Ask each team member to share and discuss their answers on the *Process Review* form.

9. The facilitator concludes the session with a discussion on the learnings from the activity and a lecturette on consensus decision making. See Activity 45, The Effective Team Member: A Consensus Activity, for guidelines for reaching a consensus.

164

RANKING SHEET

	1 YOUR INDIVIDUAL RANKING	2 THE TEAM'S RANKING	3 EXPERT'S RANKING	4 DIFFERENCE BETWEEN STEP 1 & 3	5 DIFFERENCE BETWEEN STEP 2 & 3
1. Agricultural worker					
2. Police officer					
3. Deep sea diver					
4. Construction worker					
5. Cattle farmer					
6. Welder					
7. Chemical worker					
8. Miner					
9. Trawler person					
10. Firefighter					
TOTAL SCORES				YOUR SCORE	TEAM SCORE

165

ANSWER SHEET

1. Deep sea diver

2. Trawler person

3. Miner

4. Construction worker

5. Agricultural worker

6. Welder

7. Chemical worker

8. Police officer

9. Firefighter

10. Cattle farmer

From: *The People's Almanac*, 1988

CONSENSUS DECISION-MAKING PROCESS REVIEW

Reflect on this activity for a few minutes.

1. What helped the team reach a consensus?

2. What hindered the team?

3. What should the *team* do to increase its effectiveness in arriving at a consensus?

4. What can *you* do to increase the effectiveness of the team in arriving at a consensus?

167

Activity 42
QUESTIONS WE ASK OURSELVES

Purpose

To help a team reflect on their purpose, structure, and rewards.

Group Size

Works best with an intact team of four to eight people.

Time

Two hours.

Physical Setting

A conference table and chairs in a room large enough for the group to work comfortably.

Materials

Copy of the *Questions We Ask Ourselves (QWAO) Form* for each person.

Process

1. The team leader distributes the *QWAO Form* and asks the team members to complete it.
2. Each team member then shares his/her answer to the first question with the entire team. A general discussion follows.
3. Step 2 is repeated for remaining questions.
4. The team leader conducts a general reflective discussion of the entire team's responses and engages in an action planning process to deal with the needs identified.

© Parker and Kropp, 1992. Published by Kogan Page.

Variations

1. Members complete the *QWAO* prior to the session.

2. Responses are collected from other members of the organization.

3. Another team assessment activity is Activity 15, Characteristics of an Effective Work Team.

QUESTIONS WE ASK OURSELVES

Directions: To start on the path to developing a High Performing Team, the following seven questions require pondering (and answers!):

1. What are we here to do?

2. How shall we organize ourselves?

3. Who is in charge?

4. Who cares about our success?

5. How do we work through problems?

6. How do we fit in with other groups?

7. What benefits do the team members need from the team?

Activity 43
TEAM CONFLICT MODE

Purpose

1. To learn the five modes of dealing with conflict.
2. To identify your team's dominant conflict mode.
3. To improve your team's ability to use the collaborative mode.

Group Size

Works best with an intact team of four to eight people. Can be adapted for use in a team training workshop with a larger group.

Time

Two hours.

Physical Setting

With an intact team, a conference table and chairs.

Materials

1. Copies of *Conflict Management Mode* chart and *Conflict Management Mode Definitions* for each person.
2. An easel, flip chart, and markers.

Process

1. Explain the purpose of the activity. Distribute a copy of the *Conflict Management Mode*. Review and explain each method of dealing with conflict. Ask the team for examples of each method.
2. Working individually, each team member plots his/her perception of the team's dominant mode on the grid.
3. The leader draws a large copy of the grid on the flip chart. Each person places a dot on the grid indicating his/her perception of the team's conflict mode. The team discusses the various perceptions.

173

4. The session concludes with a consensus on ways the team can move toward collaboration as the team's dominant mode of conflict management.

Variations

1. Team members can plot their personal conflict mode, present their perception to the group, and receive feedback from the rest of the team.

2. Two interdependent teams can meet and use the *Conflict Management Mode* to plot their perceptions of the other team's dominant mode.

3. For an exercise that focuses on individual conflict styles, see Activity 17, Communicating About Conflict.

CONFLICT MANAGEMENT MODE

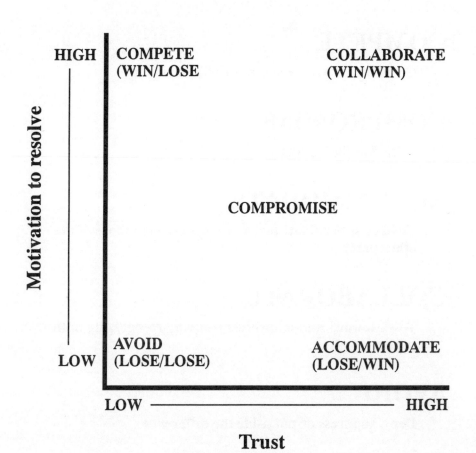

CONFLICT MANAGEMENT MODE
DEFINITIONS

COMPETE

Go all out to win; concern for objectives only

COMPROMISE

Settle for "half a loaf"

ACCOMMODATE

Yield or subordinate one's own concerns to those of the other party

COLLABORATE

Work toward mutual problem-solving recognizing both parties' goals

AVOID

Deny, suppress or put aside the difference

176

Activity 44

THAT'S ME: A GET ACQUAINTED ACTIVITY

Purpose

1. To help team members interact by sharing values.
2. To help participants get acquainted quickly.
3. To introduce the characteristics of team players.

Group Size

Unlimited. The activity can be used in a team building session with an intact team and in a team training workshop.

Time

Thirty to forty-five minutes.

Physical Setting

A large room with blank walls suitable for posting flip chart paper.
A chair for each person.

Materials

Easel, flip chart, markers, Sellotape or drawing pins.

Process

1. Prior to the session the facilitator prepares flip chart sheets with team player descriptions printed with large, clear letters. The sheets are posted on the wall at various points around the room. Chairs are positioned in a circle under each piece of paper. See *Team Player Characteristics* for ideas for the descriptions.
2. Explain the purpose of the activity. Ask participants to move to the chart that presents a characteristic which best describes them.
3. When groups are formed under the charts, ask people to discuss why they selected the characteristics and what types of things they do on their team that reflect the characteristic.

4. Ask people to move to another chart that also describes them. Ask them to share the same types of things as in step 3.

5. If time permits, ask people to move again and have the same discussion.

6. Bring the total group together. Lead a summary discussion on learning from the activity.

Variations

1. Change the characteristics to reflect issues in the group or the goals of the workshop.

2. After the people have discussed the characteristic, they can introduce themselves to each other.

3. After the people have discussed the characteristic, they can be given a problem to solve.

4. Other get acquainted activities are Activity 21, Darts; Activity 2, Yea Team!; and Activity 27, Forming New Teams.

178

TEAM PLAYER CHARACTERISTICS

DEPENDABLE

ORGANIZED

LOGICAL

FLEXIBLE

FORWARD-LOOKING

VISIONARY

INFORMAL

SUPPORTIVE

ENCOURAGING

CANDID

ETHICAL

ADVENTUROUS

Activity 45

THE EFFECTIVE TEAM MEMBER: A CONSENSUS ACTIVITY

Purpose

1. To learn the characteristics of the effective team member.
2. To learn the techniques of reaching a consensus decision.
3. To learn how to observe team dynamics.

Group Size

A training exercise for a group of up to twenty people.

Time

Two hours.

Physical Setting

A training room with two sets of chairs arranged in a circle. The result is a circle within a circle.

Materials

A copy of *Characteristics of an Effective Team Member*, *Guidelines for Reaching a Consensus*, and *Observation Guide* for each person.

Process

1. Divide the group in half. A simple way to do this is to go around the group having them count off "1,2,1,2..."
2. Have the "1's" form the inner circle and the "2's" form the outer circle. Each person from the outer circle is teamed up with one person from the inner circle. These teams of two meet briefly to have the inner circle person identify some team member skills he/she wants to improve and wants the outer circle person to observe.

181

3. The outer circle people are given the *Observation Guide* to use as a guide to observing the inner group. Under "other" they should add the skills their partner wants to improve.

4. The inner group is given the *Characteristics of an Effective Team Member*. They are asked to rank the characteristics in order of their importance to team effectiveness. Then they are asked to discuss and come up with a team consensus on the ranking of the characteristics. The time limit is 30 to 45 minutes.

5. The inner circle members meet with their outer circle partner to discuss and receive feedback on their participation with special emphasis on the areas they wanted to improve.

6. The outer circle team then gives general feedback to the inner group on the exercise. The facilitator leads a discussion on how to reach a consensus. The handout, *Guidelines for Reaching a Consensus*, is distributed and reviewed.

7. The session concludes with a discussion of the characteristics of an effective team member and the implications for the back-home teams of the participants in the workshop.

Variations

1. Have members of the inner circle role play specific team member characteristics. This would eliminate the observation feature of the activity where the outer circle person observes the behaviour of one person in the inner circle. The observers would focus just on the team dynamics.

2. Extend the exercise by reversing the circles and having the outer circle move to the inner circle and vice versa.

3. Have the outer group become the inner circle and discuss the consensus activity they just observed. The new outer circle becomes the observers of the inner circle. The new outer circle then provides feedback on the discussion they have just observed.

4. Distribute *Guidelines for Reaching a Consensus* **prior** to the team consensus exercise. The team is instructed to use the guidelines during the exercise.

5. See Activity 41, Tough Jobs, for another consensus activity.

CHARACTERISTICS OF AN EFFECTIVE TEAM MEMBER

Please rank the characteristics according to their importance to the success of the team. Each member of the team is to individually rank the items, starting with "1" as the most important, to "10" as the least important.

After everyone has finished the individual ranking, rank the 10 items as a team.

Individual	Characteristics	Team
_____	Does homework/comes prepared	_____
_____	Arrives on time	_____
_____	Shares information/ideas	_____
_____	Asks questions	_____
_____	Listens	_____
_____	Challenges assumptions	_____
_____	Refocuses discussions	_____
_____	Summarizes	_____
_____	Harmonizes conflicts	_____

GUIDELINES FOR REACHING A CONSENSUS

- Listen carefully and be open to different ideas.
- Avoid changing your mind simply to avoid conflict.
- Do not vote.
- Do not "horse trade."
- Welcome differences of opinion.

You have reached a consensus when . . .

- Your point of view has been fully heard and considered by the team.
- You have considered everyone else's point of view.
- You can "live" with the decision and will support it.

OBSERVATION GUIDE: TEAM MEMBER CHARACTERISTICS

Shares information and ideas:

Asks questions:

Is open to new ideas:

Used good listening skills (e.g., paraphrasing):

Challenges assumptions:

Supports contributions of others:

Refocuses discussions (keeps us on track):

Summarizes the discussion:

Harmonizes conflict:

Other:

Activity 46
CREATING A TEAM LOGO

Purpose

1. To initiate or conclude a discussion of team values and purpose.
2. To open or close a team building or training workshop with an energizing activity.

Group Size

Works best with an intact team of four to twelve people. The activity can be used in team training workshop when the group has been divided into teams.

Time

Forty-five minutes to one hour.

Physical Setting

For a team building session, chairs are arranged in a circle or around a conference table. In a team training workshop, round or rectangular tables, and chairs spread out around the room.

Materials

Easel, flip charts, markers, Sellotape or drawing pins.

Process

1. Explain that the purpose of the activity is to create a logo for the team. The logo is to represent their team values, purpose and anything else that distinguishes the team. Suggest that they begin the activity with a discussion of their values, purpose, etc. The finished product is to be presented on a sheet of flip chart paper.
2. The team presents the logo along with its rationale. In a team training workshop, other teams may ask questions for clarification. The facilitator may ask the team to share their learnings from the experience.

3. The team may elect to take the logo back to the workplace and use it in some fashion.

Variations

1. Create a team slogan, song or name.
2. Select a well-known song, movie, television show or book which reflects the team's purpose and/or values (e.g., *Anything Goes, You'll Never Walk Alone, The Commitments.*

188

Activity 47
I'M GONNA SIT RIGHT DOWN AND WRITE MYSELF A LETTER

Purpose

1. To summarize the key learnings from a team building or team training session.
2. To close a team building or training session on a positive note.
3. To provide the basis for on-the-job follow up of a team building or training session.

Group Size

Unlimited.

Time

Thirty minutes.

Physical Setting

1. For a team building session, chairs set up around a conference table.
2. For a tream training workshop, chairs and tables arranged in a U-shape or groupings of rectangular tables and chairs spread around the room.

Materials

Pens, stationery and envelopes for each person. Postage stamps will be required at a later date.

Process

1. Explain the purpose of the activity. You may wish to sing the title song of the activity.
2. Distribute materials.

3. Ask each person to write him/herself a letter that summarizes key learnings from the session. Explain that the letter will be sent to them in two weeks. Therefore, they should include things in the letter they want to be reminded of (e.g., personal action plan, new skills/knowledge, team goals). The letter should be placed in the envelope and sealed. The envelope should be self addressed.

4. The facilitator should collect all the envelopes.

5. Two weeks later the envelopes should be mailed.

Variations

1. Change the two-week time period to a period that is appropriate for the session.

2. The content of the letter can be specific to the purpose of the session.

190

Activity 48
INTERDEPENDENT IMAGES

Purpose

1. To understand the interdependence between work teams.
2. To explore the perceptions that interdependent teams have about one another.

Group Size

Two or more work teams that have a high level of interdependence. Works best with teams of four to twelve people.

Time

Two hours.

Physical Setting

A large room for the entire group and two smaller areas for groups to work separately.

Materials

Easel, flip chart, markers and Sellotape or drawing pins.

Process

1. The facilitator explains the purpose and logistics of the meeting.
2. Each team meets separately for about 30- 45 minutes to generate data to answer the following questions:

    a. What do we need from group X to achieve our goals?

    b. What do we owe group X so that they can achieve their goals?

    The goal of the meetings is to achieve clarity around the level of inter-dependence among the two teams.

3. The teams reassemble and each reports its work.

191

4. The groups meet again separately to prepare responses to the data presented.

5. The teams reassemble for a third time and report the product of their work. The discussion should lead to an understanding of the requirements of interdependence. The final product is a contract between the teams to follow after the meeting.

Variations

1. Teams can be asked to come prepared with a list of things required from the other team.

2. Step 4 can be changed to form mixed teams to respond to the data.

Activity 49
SOS: AN OD INTERVENTION

Purpose

1. To assess the degree to which your organization supports teamwork as business strategy.

2. To identify the supports required for the success of teamwork as a business strategy.

3. To develop a plan enhancing the organizational supports for teamwork as a business strategy.

Group Size

Works best with a team of four to eight people.

Time

Six hours. May be divided into two or three short sessions.

Physical Setting

A small room with a conference table and chairs.

Materials

1. A copy of *Survey of Organizational Supports (SOS)* for each person.

2. An easel, flip chart, markers, Sellotape or drawing pins.

Process

1. Prior to the meeting, distribute the *Survey* to a representative sample of employees in the organization. Summarize the results and prepare a report for use by the team.

2. At the meeting, isolate the key factors that need to be improved in order to increase the support for teamwork. Discuss examples of the current supports and factors working against teamwork. Try to work on only a few issues at a time.

193

3. Develop an action plan for each of the issues. If appropriate, use the *Team Action Plan*.

Variations

1. Revise the *SOS* to include factors that are more closely related to your organization.

2. Revise *SOS* to include a space for respondents to write in examples of the support (e.g., preparing an agenda, dealing with conflict).

SURVEY OF ORGANIZATIONAL SUPPORTS (SOS)

Directions: Please indicate the degree to which you agree with the following statements. Circle one number.

	STRONGLY DISAGREE	DISAGREE	NEITHER AGREE NOR DISAGREE	AGREE	STRONGLY AGREE
1. Our vision/values/mission statement includes teamwork as a key business strategy.	1	2	3	4	5
2 Teamwork is a prominent part of all statements, presentations, and reports of our organization.	1	2	3	4	5
3. The management team of our organization encourages everyone to work as a team.	1	2	3	4	5
4. Promotions, key assignments, and projects go to people who are positive team players.	1	2	3	4	5
5. The performance appraisal system incorporates team player behaviours as important factors in assessing employee performance.	1	2	3	4	5
6 Individual performance on cross-functional teams is included in the performance appraisal prepared by the functional department manager.	1	2	3	4	5
7. The formal awards programme acknowledges the contributions of team players and teams.	1	2	3	4	5
8. Informal, day-to-day recognition regularly acknowledges the contributions of team players and teams.	1	2	3	4	5

195

	STRONGLY DISAGREE	DISAGREE	NEITHER AGREE NOR DISAGREE	AGREE	STRONGLY AGREE
9. The recruitment and hiring procedures support our efforts to increase the quantity and quality of team players in our organization.	1	2	3	4	5
10. The stories and myths which underline the norms in our organization demonstrate positive support for teamwork.	1	2	3	4	5
11. The formal work environment (space and equipment) makes it easy for teams to be successful.	1	2	3	4	5
12. The informal work environment is relaxed, casual, and encouraging of spontaneous teamwork.	1	2	3	4	5
13. The organization's planning process requires the involvement of work teams in the development of the plans.	1	2	3	4	5
14. Teams have an important place in the organization's formal structure.	1	2	3	4	5

Strengths (Factors That Support Teamwork)

Areas for Improvement (Factors That Need To Be Improved)

Activity 50
IMPROVING TEAM MEETINGS

Purpose

1. To learn the factors involved in a successful team meeting.

2. To assess the current strengths of your team meetings.

3. To develop a plan for improving your team meetings.

Group Size

Works best with an intact team of four to twelve people. The activity can be adapted to a team training workshop for a larger group.

Time

Two hours.

Physical Setting

Conference table with chairs for a session with an intact team. The room arrangement for a training workshop will depend on the size of the group.

Materials

A copy of the *Team Meeting Survey* form.

Process

1. Prior to the session, ask each team member to complete the form. Summarize the results and prepare a report for use at the session.

2. Distribute the results. Discuss and clarify the results.

3. Identify the key items that need to improve. Develop a series of action plans to address the key items.

4. Summarize the meeting and next steps.

197

Variations

1. Revise the *Survey* or use only a portion of it.
2. The facilitator can observe a team meeting and include his/her observations in the diagnosis.
3. Use the results as a basis for training sessions on specific aspects of a team meeting.

THE TEAM MEETING SURVEY

Please think about the meetings your team conducts. Using the following scale, assess the extent to which these statements are true:

5 ALMOST ALWAYS
4 OFTEN
3 SOMETIMES
2 RARELY
1 ALMOST NEVER

STATEMENTS	ALMOST ALWAYS	OFTEN	SOMETIMES	RARELY	ALMOST NEVER
1. Meetings are held only when necessary.	1	2	3	4	5
2. Effective use is made of non-meeting methods (e.g., conference calls).	1	2	3	4	5
3. There is an agenda for the meeting.	1	2	3	4	5
4. Participants receive the agenda prior to the meeting.	1	2	3	4	5
5. Agenda topics are sufficiently clear and specific.	1	2	3	4	5
6. Each agenda item specifies the time allocated to it.	1	2	3	4	5
7. Each agenda item specifies the person responsible for it.	1	2	3	4	5
8. The meeting notice includes the time the meeting will end.	1	2	3	4	5
9. The meeting notice specifies the pre-work required for the meeting.	1	2	3	4	5
10. The agenda specifies the action required on each item.	1	2	3	4	5
11. Only the necessary and appropriate people attend the meeting.	1	2	3	4	5
12. Where possible, meetings are scheduled at the best possible time (i.e., time of day, day of week).	1	2	3	4	5

	ALMOST ALWAYS	OFTEN	SOMETIMES	RARELY	ALMOST NEVER
13. A sufficient number of breaks are built into the schedule of long meetings.	1	2	3	4	5
14. The right number of people attend the meeting.	1	2	3	4	5
15. The room arrangement is appropriate for the purpose of the meeting.	1	2	3	4	5
16. Prior to the meeting, the room is checked to ensure the arrangement is acceptable and the equipment is in working order.	1	2	3	4	5
17. Participants do their homework and come prepared for the meeting.	1	2	3	4	5
18. As appropriate, outside speakers and other resources are invited to the meeting.	1	2	3	4	5
19. Effective use is made of presentation equipment (e.g., overhead projector).	1	2	3	4	5
20. The meeting is opened with a brief statement of the purpose and review of the agenda.	1	2	3	4	5
21. The meeting starts on time.	1	2	3	4	5
22. As appropriate, the agenda serves as a guide for conducting the meeting.	1	2	3	4	5
23. Members are encouraged to participate in the discussions.	1	2	3	4	5
24. Effective use is made of questions to clarify ideas; bring out opinions; and in other ways, manage the discussion.	1	2	3	4	5
25. Differences of opinion are explored and resolved effectively.	1	2	3	4	5
26. Team members demonstrate good listening skills.	1	2	3	4	5

	ALMOST ALWAYS	OFTEN	SOMETIMES	RARELY	ALMOST NEVER
27. Discussions are summarized at various points during the meeting.	1	2	3	4	5
28. The group is encouraged to see a consensus on key decisions.	1	2	3	4	5
29. The discussions stay focused on the issue under consideration.	1	2	3	4	5
30. Problem participants are dealt with effectively.	1	2	3	4	5
31. The team celebrates the achievement of milestones and other successes.	1	2	3	4	5
32. Individual members receive recognition for contributions.	1	2	3	4	5
33. The team is open and honest in assessing the quality of its work.	1	2	3	4	5
34. Team members are willing to pitch in and help each other out.	1	2	3	4	5
35. As appropriate, the team takes the time to revisit its overall mission and goals.	1	2	3	4	5
36. The efficiency of team meetings is enchanced by the use of subgroups and committees.	1	2	3	4	5
37. Key decisions and agreements are summarized at the end of the meeting.	1	2	3	4	5
38. Follow-up action items are agreed upon and noted.	1	2	3	4	5
39. Team members take specific responsibility for action items.	1	2	3	4	5
40. As appropriate, the date and time of the next meeting is set.	1	2	3	4	5

	ALMOST ALWAYS	OFTEN	SOMETIMES	RARELY	ALMOST NEVER
41. As appropriate, minutes are taken that summarize the key facts about the meeting and important action items.	1	2	3	4	5
42. Following the meeting, the minutes are distributed to team members in a reasonable amount of time.	1	2	3	4	5
43. The meetings end on time.	1	2	3	4	5
44. The leader communicates with team members between meetings about important issues or problems raised during the meeting.	1	2	3	4	5

Comments

A.   Strengths: What aspects of the meetings are handled well?

B.   Weaknesses: What areas need improvement?